Class Meetings

Building Leadership, Problem-Solving and
Decision-Making Skills
in the Respectful Classroom

Donna Styles

Pembroke Publishers Limited

To Geoff and Melanie,
who will make a tremendous
difference in the lives of
children

And to Mel,
who already does

© **2001 Pembroke Publishers**
538 Hood Road
Markham, Ontario, Canada L3R 3K9
www.pembrokepublishers.com

Distributed in the U.S. by Stenhouse Publishers
477 Congress Street
Portland, ME 04101
www.stenhouse.com

We acknowledge the financial support of the Government of Canada through the Book Publishing Industry Development Program (BPIDP) for our publishing activities.

National Library of Canada Cataloguing in Publication Data

Styles, Donna
    Class meetings: building leadership, problem-solving and decision-making skills in the respectful classroom

Includes bibliographical references and index.
ISBN 1-55138-134-6

    1. Classroom management.   2. Meetings.   3. Group problem solving.   4. Decision making in children. I. Title.

LB3013.S79 2001   372.1102'4   C2001-901388-4

Cover photo taken in Jim Dart's class at Wells Street Public School.

Editor: Jennifer Drope
Proofreader: Lori Burak
Cover Design: John Zehethofer
Cover Photo: Ajay Photographics
Typesetting: Jay Tee Graphics Ltd.

Printed and bound in Canada
9 8 7 6 5 4 3 2 1

Contents

Preface

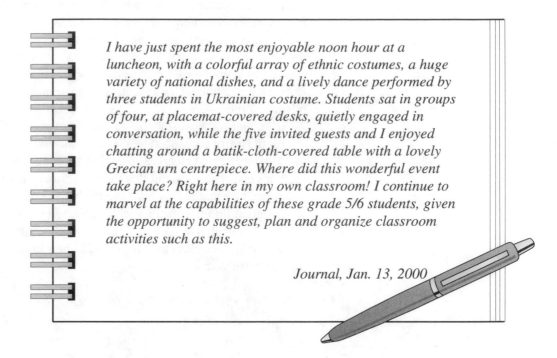

I have just spent the most enjoyable noon hour at a luncheon, with a colorful array of ethnic costumes, a huge variety of national dishes, and a lively dance performed by three students in Ukrainian costume. Students sat in groups of four, at placemat-covered desks, quietly engaged in conversation, while the five invited guests and I enjoyed chatting around a batik-cloth-covered table with a lovely Grecian urn centrepiece. Where did this wonderful event take place? Right here in my own classroom! I continue to marvel at the capabilities of these grade 5/6 students, given the opportunity to suggest, plan and organize classroom activities such as this.

Journal, Jan. 13, 2000

The original idea for a potluck was suggested at a class meeting, and within minutes, the students had decided that a multicultural theme would fit well with our current social studies unit on immigration, and that we could celebrate Canada's mosaic of cultures with food from different countries. Ideas then came fast and furious—dressing up in ethnic costumes, labeling the dishes with the country of origin, inviting guests (e.g., the principal, the librarian, the learning assistance teacher), bringing their own placemats, dishes and cutlery, and striking up a committee to put it all together.

Meetings like these are energizing for me as a teacher. Watching your students involved in the goings-on of their classroom is always inspiring, and when students are also involved in making decisions about classroom activities, their sense of ownership and their feeling of community is greatly increased.

Although I had always involved my students in discussions on various topics and had conducted informal class meetings in the early 1970s, the idea of holding weekly class meetings with a more formalized problem-solving process did not occur to me until the late 80s. For a number of years, my husband and I had held family meetings with our own two children. We saw how positive these meetings were in creating a unified family feeling, in helping our children see their importance in the family unit and in making them feel that their opinions were heard and respected.

I began to think of using such a model in the classroom. At the time, I was working part-time as a resource teacher, and did not have my own class. Then, I was fortunate to join a staff where class meetings were conducted in several of the classrooms. With the help of colleagues, the family meeting philosophy, and extensive reading and research, I developed the class meeting model I currently use that is outlined in this book.

Though I have held class meetings for many years now, I continue to be amazed at what a difference they make to the tone of my classroom. Students are more cooperative with each other, they behave better, and they show more responsibility for their learning. Students feel respected, they feel they are part of the class and they are happy about coming to school. I spend far less time disciplining and more time listening to what my students have to say. I love coming to school each day because my classroom is a happy, encouraging, exciting place to be. Class meetings play a large part in the creation of this positive atmosphere.

After hearing what students say about class meetings when they are asked, I am more firmly convinced than ever about their power. Research conducted for my Masters degree clearly shows that students not only see the many benefits of regular class meetings, but that they absolutely love having them!

I hope the ideas in this book are useful to you, both in providing validation for the great things you are already doing in your classroom, and in giving you some new insights or ideas. Be patient with yourself as you learn how to conduct effective class meetings, and, when in doubt, trust your students. They will surprise you.

Donna Styles
Armstrong, BC

Introduction: Class Meetings Are a Powerful Tool

I have been an educational interpreter for the deaf for the last 13 years. My job puts me into a variety of classrooms with teachers that use many different techniques or strategies to teach children. I have never been involved in any one technique that so accomplishes the goal of social education for the student as class meetings. It covers everything that you would want a student to have mastered socially and individually: problem solving on their own, community responsibility, focusing on the positive attributes of others, taking a stand for what they believe in and fostering a spirit of cooperation in order to succeed. Class meetings to me equal what the word "empowerment" should mean in a classroom. I think this is an essential tool in every classroom.

Michelle Kuzyk, Educational Interpreter,
School District #83, Armstrong, BC

As classroom teachers today, all of us have an incredible amount on our plates. We sometimes feel overwhelmed with the many demands on our time and energy—individual learning styles to accommodate in our lesson plans, behavior problems to deal with, students with special needs to integrate, new curriculums to implement, marking, supervision, reports to write, coaching and meetings to attend. You might well ask, "How can I possibly add one more thing to my timetable?" Yes, class meetings do take one period a week, but I can attest that that one period will have more far-reaching effects than any other one thing you do.

What Is a Class Meeting?

Just sitting down in a class meeting with everyone helps you get a feel for the group and others' opinions.

Janine, age 17, reflecting on meetings when she was in grade 5

The term *class meeting* may mean different things in different classrooms and may serve a variety of purposes. In some classrooms, a class meeting is simply a time to share information with students about what is going on in the class or school that week, while in some classes, teachers gather students together to make plans for a new unit of study. Yet other teachers use class meetings to try to solve problems that come up in the class.

Some teachers hold meetings informally when the need arises to discuss something of importance with the students, while others schedule meetings on a regular basis, and use a more formalized method. Regardless of the model a teacher uses, class meetings provide students with the opportunity to participate in a group exchange of ideas in a respectful, caring atmosphere. Class meetings are a place to share, encourage, listen, think, decide, plan and evaluate.

7

The class meeting model outlined in this resource, which is the model I currently use in my classroom, has been refined and honed over the years, based on what I have found to be successful. The format is similar in many ways to a typical business meeting, but is based on the creative problem-solving process frequently found in higher-level thinking skills programs, and incorporates elements of numerous models cited in literature on the subject.

What Are the Characteristics of the Model Proposed in This Book?

The class meeting model outlined in this book includes several key components which make it unique and effective:

- Students sit on chairs in a circle
- Meetings are held every week
- Students lead the meetings
- Both problems and suggestions are discussed
- Students encourage and compliment each other
- A set format for the meeting is followed each week

What Are the Purposes of Class Meetings?

Class meetings have a great impact on the students and the tone of the classroom. The following are some of the main purposes for which class meetings are useful.

1. Class meetings assist students in personal growth—Class meetings provide a forum for student voice in the classroom; a place where ideas can be heard in the respectful atmosphere of a circle. When students see that their ideas are listened to and not laughed at, they begin to feel more comfortable speaking in front of the group. Frequent encouragement from their classmates helps them to see themselves as lovable, capable and responsible individuals. Self-esteem is nurtured and self-confidence increases.

2. Class meetings help students to resolve conflict—Students bring problems to the meeting that they wish to have help in solving. The group must then work hard to clarify problems before it comes up with possible solutions. With so many practices at using a formalized problem-solving model, students begin to internalize the process, and are better able to solve problems on their own.

3. Class meetings allow students to make suggestions and plan activities— Class meetings not only serve the purpose of problem resolution, but also provide an opportunity for students to suggest activities that the class might do. This gives students the chance to work on committees and organize events. Students feel an increased sense of ownership of their classroom as they are given the responsibility for making decisions and carrying them out.

4. Class meetings help improve academics—When students feel valued, they are happier, and when they are happy, they like coming to school. As students notice each other's progress and strengths, they begin to take more pride in a job well done. The more self-confident and supported students feel, the more effort they put into their work. Success breeds success. With increased effort and enthusiasm, marks improve, and a noticeable difference is made in the student's academic standing.

We haven't had any problems lately and that means either that our class is getting better at solving problems on their own or they're just trying harder not to get into fights.

Student, age 11

8

5. *Class meetings unify the class*—As conflicts in the class are resolved and feelings are shared, friction is reduced. At this point, the class begins to function as a community, working together toward goals and showing support for all members. Students feel a sense of belonging to the group, and the tone in the classroom becomes very positive and caring.

6. *Class meetings serve as a classroom management tool*—When students are accountable to their peers, misbehavior in the classroom is reduced, and when it does occur, deciding upon consequences is a shared responsibility of both the class and the teacher. Many misbehaviors disappear as students begin to use strategies they have investigated in meetings. As the members of the class group accept the "rules" and expectations of their peers, students begin to monitor their own behavior and become better self-managers, reducing the need for teacher intervention. The class becomes more cooperative, and routines and expectations are willingly followed.

7. *Class meetings offer a forum for recognizing and celebrating class accomplishments*—When one individual helps another or a group performs an appreciated task; when the class reaches a goal it has set or is working hard to achieve one; when students are proud of something they have accomplished; or when someone just wants to say "thanks for being my friend"—all of these can be recognized at class meetings, and more. In class meetings, students celebrate their growth, their learning and their successes, and in the process, they learn to verbalize their appreciation by giving and receiving compliments in an appropriate manner.

8. *Class meetings provide an occasion for enjoying each other's company*—Although class meetings are serious business, laughter can often be heard at meetings. The process is formal, but the atmosphere is relaxed, comfortable and accepting. Students and adults alike enjoy sharing funny incidents or comments that come up, and there is a real feeling of camaraderie in the group.

What Skills Do Students Gain?

In addition to meeting students' emotional and social needs, participating in the process of class meetings develops many other important skills in students, including:

- Listening skills
- Responding skills
- Public-speaking skills
- Leadership skills
- Organizational skills
- Thinking skills
- Problem-solving skills

Many of these areas are discussed in more detail in the next chapter.

What Grades Can Class Meetings Be Conducted In?

I have used meetings very successfully in grades 3 to 6 (students ages 8 to 12), but many of my colleagues have held similar meetings with younger students (ages 5 to 8), and older students (ages 12 and 13). It is also possible to hold meetings with students in the middle school grades and into secondary school.

The model in this book can be modified and changed to meet the needs of any group. However, there are several important characteristics which contribute to the success of class meetings in achieving many goals and learning outcomes, regardless of age. These include:

- Holding meetings at a regular time each week
- Sitting in a circle where everyone can see each other
- Training students to lead the meetings
- Following a problem-solving process and consistent format

What Is in This Book?

The class meeting model outlined and explained in this book is offered as a starting place for the novice who has never conducted meetings, as well as a resource for teachers experienced in conducting meetings who may be looking for fresh ideas or for answers to questions regarding their own meetings.

Before utilizing a new idea in the classroom, teachers must believe in its value, thinking that it will make an appreciable difference to their classroom. Chapter 1 discusses the specific effects class meetings have on the students, the teacher and the tone of the classroom. It shows which learning outcomes class meetings target in various curriculum areas.

In Chapter 2, the class meeting model is outlined, with each section of the meeting explained. Chapter 3 then illustrates the steps necessary for getting ready for meetings, with specific lessons suggested for use in preparing students for the process. Finally, Chapter 4 provides detailed information to help teachers answer specific concerns regarding meetings, and to assist in making meetings run smoothly.

The importance of creating a positive affective atmosphere in the classroom to support class meetings is clarified in Chapter 5, and various activities which foster both individual growth and group dynamics are offered.

Chapter 6 discusses the use of several assessment tools and informal methods that can help provide feedback on the effectiveness of class meetings. Also included are some ideas for special activities to do with students that celebrate their experience together as a class.

A Powerful Tool

I think that class meeting is a wonderful thing to do. It helps kids a lot with their problems. Also, it is a fun way to make a committee and it is also very groupy. I love class meetings because everyone is involved and it is a class project. I really love class meetings, and I really hope that lots of classes will learn how to do class meetings.

Student, age 10

I believe my students to be the biggest fans of class meetings, experiencing for themselves their value. It is for this reason that I have sprinkled this resource with their comments, written originally in reflective journals or given in interviews. Except for three high school students asked about their experience with class meetings when they were younger, comments are from boys and girls in grades 3 to 6, ranging in age from 8 to 12.

All students come to school wanting to succeed, to get along well in their studies and with others, and to have friends. Class meetings go a long way toward helping students achieve this, and are a powerful tool for any teacher to use. Class meetings help a good classroom to be even better. The true power of meetings lies in their ability to empower students, to motivate them to learn, and to help them discover their personal best. What better endorsement than this comment made by one student who said: *In class meetings, the class brings it out. I mean, they bring the whole spirit of the class into the circle. I think class meetings are powerful because it brings the best out of you.*

1

Why Class Meetings?

Being able to build consensus in a school or a classroom (or a family) takes time. It also takes work and commitment ... and some definite communication skills. It requires folks to understand their "position" and the great need for flexibility in moving from that position. And I believe it is one of the new "basic skills" that citizens of our society need right now. I think we agree with this "philosophically" ... it's the putting it into practice that is more difficult. One way that I have found helpful to teach consensus-building skills to students is through the use of class meetings.

Dr. Dawn Benson, Director of Instruction,
School District #83, Salmon Arm, BC

Class meetings affect the very fabric of a classroom. Literature on the topic of class meetings, and the vast accounting of personal experiences by educators using them shows a definite agreement about the positive effects these meetings have. Class meetings are viewed as being the cornerstone of democratic classrooms, fostering both affective and cognitive growth in students, and impacting the class as a whole. They can play a critical role in the development of students':

- Emotional development
- Social development
- Moral development
- Intellectual development

Students become more responsible for both their learning and their behavior when they feel they are given choices and are allowed to make decisions. The benefits extend beyond the students to include the classroom teacher, as well as parents. In classrooms where class meetings are conducted effectively, students monitor their own, and each other's, behavior, allowing the teacher to enjoy the classroom without having to constantly fill the role of "policeperson."

It makes me go out and try my hardest after class meetings.

Student, age 10

Students who have a say in their classroom, who are involved in planning activities, who are working together to reach goals and who feel valued and encouraged by their peers, look forward to coming to school. Enthusiastic, happy students feel successful and they try harder, often resulting in improvements to their academics. When parents see that their children have a positive attitude toward school, and they are succeeding, they too are happy, knowing that all is well with their children at school.

This chapter discusses the benefits of class meetings in five main areas:

- Personal growth
- Leadership, organizational and public-speaking skills
- Thinking skills and cognitive gains
- Problem-solving skills
- Interpersonal skills for creating a community of learners

Personal Growth

One thing I find really different about these class meetings than my old school's class meeting is we did not do thank you and compliments and we did not encourage each other ... I like these class meetings because they are different. I think that trust is very important ... I would bring up lots of solutions if people would not laugh at me. When I first came into this class I thought that I could not trust any of the kids, but now I know I can. Class meetings are very good for a person to feel wanted.

Student, age 10

Students must like and respect themselves before they are able to interact with others in positive ways. Participating in the Encouragement Circle and Thank-you's and Compliments parts of the class meeting model outlined in this book shows students how they are seen by their peers, enhancing their awareness of their own personal profile of strengths, talents and skills. As Janine points out: *I felt more positive about myself. You realize how people see you. Maybe you never knew that about yourself before, and when they say it, you see that you are that way.*

Over the course of the school year, students improve in their ability to make positive comments to peers that boost self-esteem, and they are able to focus on the values of their peers, to notice improvements, and to recognize acts of kindness. Self-confidence grows as students feel valued as contributors to discussions and as they show responsibility in making decisions and reaching goals. A class meeting is a safe, forgiving environment where students can take risks and grow in self-exploration.

The Three-Legged Stool of Self-Confidence

1. Knowing what I do well
2. Knowing what other people appreciate about me
3. Showing I'm responsible at home or at school

(adapted from *Changes and Challenges: Becoming the Best You Can Be* by Lions Club International and Quest International)

Providing the opportunity for students to take part in respectful discussions within the class group also helps students to become more aware of their own feelings, values and opinions. Many children have not experienced the responsibility involved in formulating an opinion, defending it with valid reasons or examples, and making a decision as part of a collective. As opinions are shared and viewpoints are offered in a class meeting, students begin to discover their own feelings and thoughts on issues, helping them to clarify their own views.

Choosing solutions or plans of action at class meetings essentially forces all students to take a visible stand on the issue at hand, and to be confident in making their choice of a solution even when they may be its sole supporter. As students see their opinions being respected and supported by their peers, they gain self-esteem and become more confident contributors to discussions.

Leadership, Organizational and Public-Speaking Skills

What I remember most is the ability for the class to organize fun events. Class meetings were important because of the ability for the kids to get involved and work on their organizational skills. Leadership skills, too. For me, personally, the one thing I really remember is when we organized the 50's and 60's dance. You learn the sorts of things that need to be done to organize.

> Emily, age 17, reflecting on meetings
> when she was in grade 5

Class meetings not only enhance self-concept, but are a wonderful opportunity to develop leadership and organizational skills in students. Participation in meeting discussions improves students' public-speaking ability as well.

All of our classrooms contain outspoken students, who do not hesitate to share their ideas with the large group, but there are also those who prefer to remain quiet, and will not choose to have the spotlight solely on themselves. In the non-threatening atmosphere of class meetings, where they see that their ideas are not laughed at, quieter students gain confidence in speaking in front of a group. As trust develops, and they feel more comfortable, all students are more able not just to talk about issues, but to also share the emotions they feel around issues. According to one ten year old: *I am usually quiet about things, and when I am asked to share my opinions in meetings, I now am able to do that.*

In the silence of the circle, students see their ideas being heard and accepted, and they gain confidence in expressing themselves. All of the senior students I interviewed about their involvement with class meetings when they were many years younger mentioned improved public-speaking skills as one of the most important aspects of meetings. As Faye recalls: *It helped me with public speaking, talking in front of everybody, having the freedom to say what you think.*

Leading meetings provides the ultimate opportunity to speak in front of the group, as students are responsible for knowing what to say and do in keeping the group on track with the agenda. It is wonderful to be part of the circle when the most reserved, shy student in the class has his or her turn at chairing the meeting, and exudes confidence in his or her ability to do so. Letting students volunteer to lead the meeting when they are ready, rather than when the teacher says, allows some students the time they need to be fully comfortable with the idea, and to have internalized the process. Many students, having enjoyed receiving encouragements from everyone in the class, are surprised to find, as this student did, that: *When you are the leader, it makes you feel really special and important.*

Working on committees makes students feel responsible, and helps develop their organizational, interpersonal and leadership skills. Committee members must arrange to meet on their own time, write down ideas and decisions, and report back to the class. Depending upon the activity or event they are working

---

Learning Outcomes

Language Arts

- Participates willingly in oral activities
- Listens actively and responds verbally
- Expresses thoughts and ideas
- Communicates effectively with confidence
- Supports opinions with reasons
- Formulates questions to clarify understanding
- Expresses agreement or disagreement

Leadership Skills

- Assumes various roles in groups
- Encourages others to participate

When I was in class meeting today, I was being heard, and I felt good.

Student, age 10

on, committee members may have to make phone calls, draw up lists, interview the administrator or other adults in the school, write letters, arrange for materials or equipment to be set up, type and photocopy notices to go home, choose activities to organize and run, or make decisions regarding how certain aspects of a planned event will be executed. To do all this, they must get along as a group and be able to communicate well with each other. Jobs must be shared and delegated, and students must work together to be successful.

Thinking Skills and Cognitive Gains

My prediction is if you do class meetings over a period of years, you will get many more students motivated to learn—not just democratically, but academically.

Dr. M. Fullan, speaking on the video
Bridgette, produced by D. Benson and
J. Pippus

Students participating in effective class meetings not only benefit socially, emotionally and morally, but also intellectually. Taking part in regular class meetings with a formalized problem-solving model helps students make tremendous strides in their ability to reason, analyze, synthesize and evaluate.

Students learn that problems and solutions must be broken down into understandable parts, relationships among people and events must be considered, and plans must be organized to become a reality. Students have a chance to practise the skill of synthesizing when solutions are combined, new ideas are suggested, and they discuss the possible consequences of any new ideas. Finally, the evaluation of generated solutions to problems involves looking at criteria for possible effectiveness. For example:

- Is the solution helpful and respectful?
- Is the solution reasonable or possible?
- Are the right people responsible for making it work?
- Will the solution make a difference to the person's behavior?

When making plans for suggested activities, students must consider factors such as time, cost and personnel. Making choices, then revisiting them, helps students see the growth they are making in choosing effective solutions or the accomplishment they feel when achieving a goal or successfully carrying out a planned activity. Having to reason their way through problems, analyze data presented and generate ideas fosters cognitive growth in students.

In addition to an increased ability to think critically, students also improve in their ability to think creatively. Opportunities to create and plan activities encourages fluency, flexibility, elaboration and originality. Students improve in their ability to generate ideas when asked to brainstorm, and they see their ideas accepted in a non-evaluative manner.

One of the keys to being a good problem solver is being able to see things from a different perspective. When sharing feelings on issues, students are made to see issues from other people's point of view, helping them to be more flexible and accepting. Gathering information to clarify problems or topics increases students' ability to elaborate, and to add the details necessary for a fuller understanding. Original thinking is challenged when students must come up with innovative solutions or unique activities. As they practise using both

---

Learning Outcomes

Language Arts

- Generates and shapes ideas
- Develops questions
- Summarizes ideas
- Makes inferences
- Makes predictions
- Evaluates information

Social Studies

- Identifies a problem or issue
- Generates information
- Supports a position with reasons
- Assesses an issue from various perspectives
- Evaluates the credibility and reliability of sources

I learned today that class meetings really get you thinking.

Student, age 11

I liked that everyone kept getting new ideas very quickly, faster than last time.

Student, age 10

critical and creative thinking skills during meetings, their ability to solve problems and organize events improves as the year goes on.

Critical Thinking Skills

- Analysis—looking at parts, relationships, organization
- Synthesis—creating new; predicting consequences
- Evaluation—ranking; using criteria to make choices

Creative Thinking Skills

- Fluency—lots of ideas
- Flexibility—point of view
- Elaboration—adding details
- Originality—uniqueness

Creative Problem Solving

- Identify the problem
- Brainstorm solutions
- Discuss solutions
- Choose a solution
- Make a plan

(adapted from School District #22 Thinking Skills/Enrichment Program in Vernon, BC)

I learned how to sit still and be patient and let other kids talk. I learned how to listen to others respectfully.

Janine, age 17

I noticed something about the responses to the problem. It seemed that the problem had answers and the answers had problems.

Student, age 11

Class meetings are the "mainstay" of R. Cramer's teaching. In *Clear the Air With Class Meetings,* she notes: *I don't have any hard data to prove it raises my students' level of achievement, but I have noticed a marked improvement in their concentration, in their tolerance and understanding of others, and in their self-discipline.* Like Cramer, I have found that class meetings improve student concentration. When expected to sit quietly for a long period of time in a focused, attentive manner, students improve in their ability to simply sit still and listen. I believe this transfers into their schoolwork, as I see students better able to stay on task not just during meetings, but at other times of the day. In an age when an increasing number of our students come to school with poor attending skills, class meetings provide a valuable arena for this skill development to take place.

Many teachers also notice an increase in the number of students who are more easily able to memorize information or facts. I find that students' oral memory improves with continued exposure to class meetings. Since the proceedings at meetings are not written down for all to see—they are simply noted in the secretary's binder—students must keep track in their heads of the information they have heard. In addition, they must make connections to what they already know, formulate new opinions, and make a mental list of brainstormed suggestions that they can refer to during the discussion phase of the meeting. Decisions are made based upon all of the information previously presented, with the expectation that students remember what has been said so they can evaluate effectively.

Students become more reflective and metacognitive with continued use of class meetings. As they investigate issues, they are pensive and thoughtful.

Being responsible for making decisions that affect the group is empowering, and students take the role seriously, carefully weighing pros and cons with circumstances before decisions are made. As students look back on what happened at meetings, remember decisions that were made, and revisit, reexamine and learn from that thinking, they improve their own thinking.

Problem-Solving Skills

I learn a lot from class meeting. It gives you a chance to grow up a little. It gives you a chance to solve problems on your own instead of going to the teacher about a problem. You learn to deal with your own problems. If I was talking to a teacher or a student who had never had a class meeting before, I would tell them that it is a very good idea. It helps a lot! That's the advice I would give them.

Student, age 8

When students take part in weekly class meetings during the course of a school year, they have over thirty practices with the creative problem-solving process. Repeated sessions greatly enhance the internalization of the skills involved in solving problems. Students become familiar with the steps in identifying a problem, clarifying the facts and feelings surrounding the problem, brainstorming solutions, choosing a solution and making a plan for implementation.

Reviewing decisions the following week to see how effective they have been teaches students the importance of evaluating how their solutions are working, and promotes the idea that sometimes problems need to be revisited and new solutions need to be tried. It also helps students to see the growth in their ability to solve problems, recognizing that solutions they have chosen and decisions they have made have been successful. The most important concept a formalized process gives students is the idea that every problem has a solution, and that they are empowered to make choices and decisions they can act upon to solve problems.

Most importantly, students begin to see how the problem-solving process learned in the meetings might be used elsewhere. They begin to apply the skills they learn to areas of their lives both in and out of the classroom. With continued exposure to problem solving, students lose their fear of conflict, and they view problems in a more positive light.

Interpersonal Skills for Creating a Community of Learners

If we want to nurture students who will grow into lifelong learners, into self-directed seekers, into the kinds of adults who are morally responsible even when someone is not looking, then we need to give them opportunities to practise making choices and reflecting on the outcomes. Responsibility means owning one's failures and successes—small, medium and large.

Evelyn Schneider, author of the article
Giving Students a Voice in the Classroom

A report from the National Center for Clinical Infant Programs, discussed in D. Goleman's *Emotional Intelligence: Why It Can Matter More Than IQ*, reminds us that a successful school experience relies not so much on how well a

---

Learning Outcomes

Language Arts/Social Studies

- Identifies and clarifies a problem, issue or inquiry
- Takes a position on a problem or issue
- Shows respect for diverse opinions
- Uses strategies to resolve conflict and solve problems
- Differentiates among problems they can solve alone and those they need help with
- Practises responsible and systematic decision making
- Sees the impact of their decisions
- Accepts responsibility for choices
- Evaluates personal decisions

Goal Setting

- Sets both short- and long-term goals
- Outlines progress in meeting goals
- Revises goals and plans when needed
- Uses resources that can help meet goals
- Makes connections among planning, time management and the ability to achieve goals

---

I like class meetings. I think they're fun and they help me learn how to solve my problems as well as other people's. I have to help solve other people's problems because I'm a peer helper and that's what I do. I think helping people solve their problems is fun. I got most of my information on being a peer helper from class meetings.

Student, age 11

child can read, as on emotional and social factors. Knowing what the expectations for behavior are, how to control impulses leading to misbehavior, how to wait, and how to follow directions are part of a list of abilities determining the level of success a child experiences in school. Goleman also points out the importance of feeling empathy and showing good listening ability in helping children to have positive experiences with others. These are behaviors that can be practised and learned.

Taking part in class meetings helps students to learn to become more empathetic to others, to learn how their peers expect them to behave, to give them strategies that help reduce impulsive behavior, and to listen attentively and wait their turn. With continued use, class meetings help to reduce bullying behaviors, as students become more accountable to their peers for their actions and are able to see how others respond to this type of behavior. I have found that this type of positive peer pressure is much more effective in modifying an offending student's behavior than the intervention of a teacher.

When involved in weekly class meetings, students get to know the other students in the class much better than they would otherwise. Actively listening to each other's problems and concerns helps them to become more understanding and accepting. As Faye, age 17, remembers: *I learned to have more empathy toward others. I remember when Sally brought up the fact that she was having some problems with not having any friends, and we talked about that. It made me realize what life was like for her.*

Many schools today are integrating students with special needs into regular classrooms, and moving away from a segregated school environment. I have found class meetings to be highly successful in helping students with special needs to feel valued and accepted by the class. These students, often seen by their peers as "different," take part in meetings just as all the other students do, giving them a feeling of equality. This does wonders for boosting self-esteem, but it also leads to the rest of the class viewing the students with special needs as "normal" kids, with thoughts, feelings and ideas just like theirs. When the other students listen to what students with special needs have to say (often interpreted by a classroom aide who works with the child), they develop a better understanding, leading to acceptance by the group. As one student noted: *Class meetings made me have respect for people in the class that I probably wouldn't have talked to otherwise.*

Sometimes, the class is just not aware of what life is like for students with special needs, or what their problems might be, and class meetings can help with this. As Janine points out: *It brings everyone together so you feel part of the classroom. When people bring up problems you may not have known it was a problem before. You learn more about the kind of problems other people are having.* I believe the huge success my students and I have experienced in integrating or mainstreaming students with special needs is due, in large part, to the inclusive power of class meetings.

The importance of building a feeling of community in classrooms is a current topic of discussion among educators. Alfie Kohn defines community as a place with a "we" feeling where one feels cared about, listened to, respected, encouraged and valued. The concept of "belonging" is widely accepted as being one of the basic needs children must satisfy before they can grow in other areas. If students are not able to fulfill this need in positive ways at school, they look elsewhere, sometimes teaming up with other students or groups that engage in less than desirable activities. With busier lifestyles, broken homes and less contact with adults at home, there is a need now, more than ever, to make our students feel like they belong.

Class meetings serve to increase students' feelings of belonging, as each class member is an important part of a meeting circle where ideas are respectfully listened to and responded to, and the climate is one of caring. When students feel they belong to the group, their level of commitment increases, and they are much more likely to accept the norms established by the group.

As students listen to each others' ideas, feelings and concerns, they begin to accept and value each other, and they begin to see how their actions affect others. Students who are named in a problem brought up at a class meeting must explain themselves to their peers, making them accountable for their actions. As they listen to the discussion that takes place around the issue, they become aware of the effects their behavior has on others, or as one young student states: *You get to learn what people don't like other people to do to them.*

Understanding that you are not alone, and that you are part of a group with established norms that expects certain behavior, is an important step in moral development, leading students to behave in more socially acceptable ways. As mentioned earlier, this type of positive peer pressure acts as a powerful catalyst for causing change in behaviors deemed unacceptable or inappropriate by the group.

As students see how the problem-solving process works in class meetings, and expand their use of successful strategies, they begin to resolve their own conflicts. Students realize that everyone has problems, not just themselves, and that they can work together to solve them. There is an increased level of cooperation in the class, both in students getting along better and in being able to work together in partnerships or groups.

The level of student self-management increases as students begin to rely less on the teacher for guidance and more on their inner convictions. Misbehavior in the class greatly decreases, creating a classroom atmosphere where learning can take place. Essentially, the better students are able to manage conflicts constructively, the less time classroom teachers have to spend on disciplining students, and the more attention they can give to the rest of the curriculum.

As the year goes on and students improve their interpersonal and problem-solving abilities, less individual problems are brought up at meetings and there are more suggestions for fun activities the class can do together. Students then enjoy taking ownership for planning and organizing suggested activities together, and when these are successful, share the feeling of accomplishment for a job well done. The tone in the classroom becomes one of cooperation, appreciation and celebration.

Giving students the responsibilities of leading meetings, solving problems, making decisions and planning events empowers students, and they begin to think of themselves as an important part of the class community. As one 10 year old so aptly put it: *It gives you a chance to be a class family.*

2   A Proposed Model for Class Meetings

I think we are lucky to have class meetings. Some teachers don't even do them, they just say to solve it yourself or go tell a supervisor. I think they are very important. Not just to solve problems, but to get to talk to your class members. It is also nice to know that our teacher is really into class meetings and gives responsibility by letting us take turns being the leader. The last time I did class meetings, which was in Grade 3, the teacher was the leader every time. Class meetings also helps solve problems way faster and better.

Student, age 11

Though sharing characteristics with many models currently used by teachers who conduct class meetings, there are several distinctive features which make the class meeting model outlined in this book unique. In this model, class meetings:

- Follow a set format
- Are held once every week
- Have the class sitting on chairs in a circle
- Are led by the students
- Require students to place their problems and suggestions in a class meeting box
- Put the teacher in the role of the secretary
- Have students stating encouragements to the meeting leader
- Expect the students to solve problems and make decisions in a formal way
- Use a creative problem-solving process
- Encourage students to plan activities and form committees

In the proposed model, although the actual content of each class meeting will vary, the format for each class meeting remains the same. After clearing their desks away and forming a circle of chairs in the centre of the room, the agenda is set by the contents of a class meeting box, into which students have put their problems and suggestions during the week. The meeting leader then follows a set order for the meeting, as follows:

1. Open the meeting
2. Encourage the leader in an Encouragement Circle
3. Discuss Old Business
4. Deal with New Business (problems and suggestions)
5. Have Thank-you's and Compliments
6. Close the meeting

The Class Meeting Agenda

A written agenda that illustrates the order of events and offers the leader a guideline for the meeting, laminated and available during meetings, helps students keep meetings on track. It also serves to provide the visual framework students need to support learning and internalize the steps used in conducting an effective meeting. The agenda is written for the students, and provides the actual verbal prompts that may be used when they conduct the meeting. A sample agenda is provided on the opposite page.

Preparing for the Meeting

Before the meeting officially opens, a number of housekeeping items need to be attended to. They include:

- Getting the secretary binder and a pen or pencil ready to take with you to the meeting
- Asking the student leader to prepare for the meeting by moving his or her desk out of the way, getting the class meeting box and agenda, and sitting at the designated leader desk
- Moving any unnecessary classroom furniture out of the way
- Telling the students to get ready for the class meeting by having everything off their desks and nothing on the floor
- Waiting for the students to be silent so that they can move their desks to the sides of the room, and then carry their chairs to their designated places in the circle
- Having the student leader put his or her chair into the circle so that you have a place to sit and do your job as secretary
- Waiting for the meeting to be called to order by the meeting leader

Suggestions for handling some of these procedures efficiently will be offered in Chapters 3 and 4.

Opening the Meeting

Class meetings are fun, especially when you're the leader!

Student, age 11

After placing his or her chair in the circle, the leader takes advantage of the time it takes for the circle to be formed to empty out the class meeting box, read the notes within, and separate them into two piles—problems and suggestions. When the group has settled and everyone is quietly waiting, the leader calls the meeting to order by saying, "I now call this meeting to order."

Class Meeting Agenda

- While everyone is getting settled, empty out the box and read each paper.
- Separate papers into problems and suggestions, and put in order by date.
- Deal with problems first, then suggestions.
- Do not read any out that are not signed.

1. CALL THE MEETING TO ORDER

- Say "I now call this meeting to order."

2. ENCOURAGEMENT CIRCLE

- Say "Today, you will be encouraging me."
- Give a minute to think.
- Choose someone who has a hand up to start, then continue around the circle.

3. OLD BUSINESS

- Say "Mrs./Mr. _____ will now report on our Old Business."
- Say "Thank you, Mrs./Mr._____."

4. NEW BUSINESS

- Read out the first problem.
- Use "Steps in Solving Problems" to help you.
- After problems, read out the first suggestion.
- Use "Steps in Discussing Suggestions" to help you.

5. THANK-YOU'S AND COMPLIMENTS

- Ask Mrs./Mr. _____ if there is time for Thank-you's and Compliments today.
- If there is, begin with the person next to you and go around the circle.

6. CLOSE MEETING

- Thank everyone for listening and participating.
- Say "Please return to your seats quietly."

The Encouragement Circle

Encouragement? That felt the best. Especially when it was from people you didn't know that well. When they gave you a compliment, it felt really good. Especially at that age, I think, you need encouragement from others.

Faye, age 17

After giving the class a minute to think, the meeting leader begins Encouragement Circle by calling on the person to the left and then going around the circle. Each member of the group is required to offer an encouraging comment about the leader. Alternatively, instead of always beginning with the person beside the leader, you may wish to have students raise hands to start and the leader can then choose who will give the first encouragement. Encouragements are then offered around the circle from that person. In either case, comments are directed only to the leader of the meeting and no one else. Comments might include such statements as:

- John, I think you're an awesome server in volleyball.
- Jane, I notice that you always put your best effort into your work.
- Roberta, I like how you cheer me up when I'm down. You're a great friend.

Encouraging comments should recognize something positive about the leader's personality and talents, or recognize areas of strength or improvement. Encouragements usually begin with stems like:

- I think ...
- I notice ...
- I like the way ...

Comments about physical appearance or material possessions are not appropriate.

As the secretary, the teacher records the names of any students who say "pass," and they get another chance to add their encouragements after the first round. Students are expected to respond the second time around, after having a little more time to think. The leader usually receives the encouragement with a thank-you.

Students are challenged, but intrigued, by the Encouragement Circle. For many, it is the first time they have articulated appreciation of someone face-to-face in front of other people. As with practice in any arena, the students become very good at giving specific encouragements to their classmates.

Old Business

After Encouragement Circle, the leader calls upon the secretary (teacher) to report on Old Business. This is the one time in the meeting where the teacher leads the discussion. During the rest of the meeting, the teacher raises a hand to speak, just as the students do. I usually begin by stating the date of the last meeting, and the name of the leader that day, with a comment such as, "We last met on (date) and (name) was the leader that day. We had (number) of problems/suggestions in the box."

Problems are then revisited one at a time, by reading each one out. The teacher begins by asking the person who put the problem in how it went during the past week. If all is well, the teacher goes on to the next item. If the solution from the week before has not worked, the problem is brought back to the table for discussion, and a new plan of action is decided upon.

After problems are dealt with, suggestions from the last meeting are read out. If a committee was formed the week before, committee members are asked if they have anything to report. At this time, updates, decisions or plans are shared with the group. Often discussion follows, with the class having the opportunity to ask committee members questions.

When each item from the previous week has been dealt with, the meeting is then turned back to the leader by saying, "That's all for Old Business, (leader name)." This portion of the meeting normally takes anywhere from one to five minutes.

New Business

Class meetings are important because they help everybody. We can get together and talk about a problem and help each other solve it.

Student, age 11

New Business is the "meat" of the meeting, and is the most time-consuming part, taking up the bulk of meeting time. Having arranged problems and suggestions according to date, the leader introduces the problems first, dealing with the items with the oldest dates first. Suggestions are read out when all problems have been dealt with, also in the order of the dates submitted.

Once the first problem is read out, the person is asked if this is still a problem. If the issue is no longer a problem, the leader asks how the person solved it. It is important for students to see themselves as capable problem solvers who are able to deal with difficulties on their own. Sometimes a problem is put into the box in anger, and it is resolved later. Knowing they are handling their own problems in productive ways validates students' capabilities and goes a long way toward giving them confidence in taking responsibility for solving problems on their own.

If the problem is still a problem, the steps for problem solving, which are introduced in the next chapter, are used. Each problem or suggestion is dealt with until time runs out. Any entries not dealt with are put back into the box to be discussed next time.

Thank-you's and Compliments

Getting compliments when I'm down really brightens up my day. They make people feel good and I'm glad that we have Thank-you's and Compliments as part of our class meeting routine if there is time!

Student, age 10

If time allows, a wonderful way to end a meeting is with Thank-you's and Compliments. After checking with the teacher to make sure there is time left for this portion of the meeting, the leader goes around the circle, taking hands that are up. Group members, including adults, may thank one or more people for something they have done in the past week, or give a compliment to one or more people. Students can be recognized for such things as their help, their contributions to the group, their ability to be a good friend, etc. This is a time where students can also compliment the whole class on a job well done, a goal that has been reached, a performance, or any aspect of school life that merits a comment. Often the students will thank or compliment the teacher or other adults that work in the classroom.

The following are the rules I use to run this portion of the meeting:

- Each student can speak only once, but can give more than one thank-you or compliment to other students if they wish
- The student receiving the thank-you or compliment can recognize it with "thank you" or "you're welcome"
- No response is necessary if more than three students are named
- The leader only goes around the circle once

Other than one taking place at the beginning of the meeting and the other at the end, there are a number of important differences between the Encouragement Circle and the Thank-you's and Compliments parts of a meeting. These are shown below.

The Differences between Encouragement Circle & Thank-you's and Compliments

1. The Encouragement Circle takes places every meeting, while Thank-you's and Compliments occurs only when time allows.
2. Encouragement Circle focuses on one person only—the leader. Thank-you's and Compliments can be directed to anyone in the group.
3. During Encouragement Circle, all students are expected to give an encouragement to the leader. They may pass once, but must make a comment when they are returned to. In Thank-you's and Compliments, contributions are optional.
4. Encouragements focus on what students can do, what they have improved in, what they are good at, and aspects of their personality that are appreciated. Thank-you's are for specific things someone has done for or with another person and compliments are recognition of goals being reached or accomplishments being made.

It is important to watch for backhanded compliments, such as "John, I would like to compliment you on the gymnastics routine you did the other day, because you never used to be good in gym." Help students understand that these types of comments are not encouraging.

As the year progresses, this part of the meeting becomes very meaningful, and students improve in their ability to both give and receive compliments and thank-you's. The "family" feeling in the classroom is greatly enhanced by this portion of class meetings, as students see themselves as part of the group, and they begin to recognize and appreciate their many accomplishments, not just as individuals, but as a class.

Closing the Meeting

I think this meeting had a big impact on the class.

Student, age 11

At the end of the meeting, the leader thanks everyone for listening and participating and asks everyone to return quietly to their places. All slips of paper with problems and suggestions that have been dealt with are thrown into the garbage, and those not discussed are returned to the box. The leader then returns the class meeting box and guideline sheets to the place they are kept in the classroom, and joins the other students in putting the room back in order. As the person who has used the leader's chair during the meeting, I return the chair to where the student sits. Students then return their desks and chairs to their original position, as well as any furniture that was moved for the meeting. As during the formation of a circle to begin the class meeting, silence is expected in this movement phase at the end of the meeting.

Some teachers like to end their class meetings with the sharing of a snack that the leader has brought, such as cookies.

Steps for Class Meetings

The Quick List

1. Tell the students to clear off their desks and prepare for the class meeting.

2. Get the secretary binder and a pen or pencil.

3. Ask the leader to get ready.

4. When the students are silent, tell them to move into the class meeting.

5. Take your place in the circle (in the leader's usual chair).

6. Wait for the meeting to be called to order.

7. The leader says, "I now call this meeting to order. Today you will be encouraging me. I'll give you a minute to think."

8. Encouragement Circle.

9. Old Business.

10. New Business.

11. Thank-you's and Compliments, if time.

12. The leader says, "Thank you for listening and participating. Please return to your seats quietly."

13. Students return desks and chairs to usual seating plan.

3 Getting Ready for Class Meetings

Before conducting your first class meeting, time must be spent during the first few weeks of school in September getting ready—with the first meeting being scheduled for early October. The designated time on your timetable to hold meetings each week can be used initially to:

- Introduce the concept of class meetings
- Introduce, teach and practise encouragement
- Teach the problem-solving process
- Introduce suggestion-making and committee work
- Practise clearing desks away and forming a circle
- Prepare materials needed for the first meeting

It is important not to rush the preparation phase when you are establishing a rapport with your class and introducing them to your classroom expectations and routines. Time is needed for activities, like those found in Chapter 5, to promote cooperation in your class and a positive affective atmosphere. As well, before beginning class meetings, it is essential that students learn how to give encouragements and how to proceed step-by-step when solving a problem. Class meetings will not be as effective, nor run as smoothly, if the initial preparatory work is done too quickly.

It is also important for students to know that consequences decided upon in meetings are not to be punitive in nature, but rather are meant to help someone learn what behavior is considered socially acceptable. The challenge is in finding solutions to problems that will not only solve problems, but are respectful to the people involved.

In some classrooms, the person who is causing a problem remains anonymous. In my class, students putting a problem into the class meeting box are required to name the person(s) who are involved, or who may be causing the problem. I believe this is important for two reasons. First, students are accountable for their actions when they must explain themselves to their peers. Second, naming the person involved provides the opportunity for the person named to verify or deny statements made by the person putting the problem into the box.

I have found that students who are named in a problem listen to the discussion that takes place around the issue, and they begin to see how their behavior affects others. This is an important step in moral development, helping students become more empathetic toward others. Research shows that bullies and students engaging in violent behavior lack empathy. Class meetings support moral development and with continued use, help to reduce bullying behaviors.

At the same time, it is important to remember that only two people are allowed to speak to the problem: the student who put the problem into the box and the person named in the problem. The rest of the class cannot add their opinions or comments; they may only pose questions to identify the problem. I find that this avoids any tattling behavior or "ganging up" that might happen. Students who know they will be listened to in a respectful manner, and feel that they are in a supportive atmosphere, are honest about their feelings and their involvement in the issue at hand. When students view the weekly class meeting as a positive, exciting place to be, and are not afraid of what might come up on the agenda each week, or what the consequences might be for a certain behavior, meetings will be eagerly anticipated.

Introducing the Concept of Class Meetings

Time must be taken to introduce the concept of class meetings to the students. Students must see "the big picture" of what meetings will look like and sound like, and recognize that the meetings will provide an opportunity to make decisions together that will affect the classroom. When students know what is expected of them, and their roles in class meetings are clearly explained, they will feel comfortable entering into meetings and will be confident of their ability to succeed. In fact, when class meetings are first introduced to your students, you will be amazed at how intrigued they are by the idea, and how eager they will be to begin.

Introduce the concept of class meetings during the first few weeks in September, at the same time that you are developing a vision with the students of what kind of a classroom they would like and establishing what the code of conduct or class bill of rights will be. It is important that students understand the cooperative nature of the meetings and the purpose for conducting them.

Before getting into the specific characteristics or components of a meeting, students need to have a clear picture of what class meetings are about and why you will be having them. The following are some ideas for introducing the concept of class meetings:

- Introduce the idea—new to many students—that in this classroom they will be deciding on many of the consequences for misbehavior that occurs. Explain that, as the teacher, you are not the only person in the class, and that you will need their expert help in figuring out what to do when problems come up. Students are immediately intrigued by this, and are anxious to find out more information!
- Tell the students that when problems arise, you expect them to try and solve the problems on their own, but that sometimes, despite several attempts at a solution, a problem doesn't go away. Explain that since a lot of brains are required to solve this type of problem, it is the perfect type of problem to be discussed at a class meeting.
- Explain that the second type of problem that might come up is not necessarily a personal problem, but something involving the class as a whole. Provide the students with several examples from previous years, such as how to decide who will sit on the couch during silent reading, or what the rules will be about the Lego bin.
- Tell the students that they will also be able to make suggestions for fun things they would like to do together as a class. Clarify that things

normally planned by teachers—for example, spirit or theme days—can be suggested and planned by them.

- Let the students know that they will be learning more about class meetings over the next couple of weeks, and that they will be holding their first meeting in about three weeks.

Introducing and Teaching Encouragement

It is great to begin meetings on a positive note. I was first introduced to the idea of an Encouragement Circle by a school counselor I worked with, and was amazed at the difference it made to my class meetings. As the person who leads the first meeting of the year, I can tell you that it is incredibly powerful and humbling to receive so many heartfelt, positive comments, delivered one after the other, from every person in the class. Talk about a boost to self-esteem! The old "warm fuzzy" format I had previously used as a way of encouraging one another was soon abandoned in favor of the Encouragement Circle portion of the meeting, and I later added the Thank-you's and Compliments section to meetings to allow for comments to be directed to anyone.

Over the years, I have become aware that adding the Encouragement Circle to meetings has had an incredible impact on the importance and effectiveness of meetings. It did much more than simply replace the "warm fuzzies," and indeed serves many purposes and targets a large number of learning outcomes. The manifold purposes of the Encouragement Circle are shown on the following pages.

In order to have a common understanding about the meaning of the word "encouragement," hold a class discussion. Note that although you will engage the thoughts of the students on the subject, you will need to have a clear idea beforehand of the possible wording you will put on the chart you write at the end of the exercise. To facilitate the class discussion, you may wish to follow this lesson sequence:

- Ask the class, "What do you think the word encouragement means?"
- Record brainstormed ideas on the chalkboard or a large piece of paper
- Discuss what each idea means, once all ideas have been presented
- Come up with a common agreement as to the meaning of the word
- Suggest that there are several characteristics of and ways to begin an encouraging comment, and record these ideas on a chart such as the one shown on this page
- Discuss the meaning of encouraging statements
- Elicit from the students and give examples yourself of what an encouragement should sound like

With experience, I have found that students are better able to generate meaningful encouragements if they have the support of a few stems to begin with. The ones I have found to be most natural for the students to use are the three listed on the chart.

It is important to note that during class meetings, when twenty-five or more comments are being made about the same person, it is sometimes hard to think of something different from what other people may have said. You want students to generate as many different comments about the leader as possible, so when introducing encouragement to them, stress that they should be specific. A generalized comment such as, "I notice you're good at Phys. Ed." makes it

---

Encouragement is ...

1. Encouragement is positive.
2. Encouragement is noticing improvement.
3. Encouragement is noticing when someone is good at something.
4. Encouragement is noticing things about someone that make them great to be around.
5. Encouragement is opened with phrases like:
   – I notice ...
   – I think ...
   – I like how ...

What I feel about encouraging in class meetings is that it makes you feel really good when someone says how good you are at something or says what they really like about you. That makes me feel really good.

Student, age 10

Purposes of the Encouragement Circle

- *To recognize the leader of the meeting*—Every member of the group, students and adults alike, is required to give an encouraging comment to the leader of the meeting, one by one, around the circle.
- *To set a positive, supportive tone for the meeting.*
- *To relax the leader*—Meeting leaders are often nervous about their performance in this new role and hearing an encouraging word from every one of their peers and the adults they work with shows their acceptance of them, giving them the confidence needed to conduct a meeting.
- *To provide an opportunity for all students to speak in front of their peers*—In Encouragement Circle, the focus is on the leader, not the whole group, providing a safer atmosphere for the less confident members of the class to share their thoughts.
- *To ensure that every student participates in the class meeting*—This is the only time during a meeting when every student is expected to participate. For quieter students, it may be the only time they speak at the meeting, as participation in all other parts of the meeting is voluntary.
- *To focus on individuals*—This helps students to learn to value each and every member of the group. Every year, we have students in our classes that are less popular than others. Taking part in the Encouragement Circle goes a long way in helping these students become more accepted by the group, as classmates listen to the many positive encouragements stated by their peers.
- *To allow for each and every student to be heard*—Being the only person speaking to a quiet, circular audience where everyone can see each other guarantees that you are being listened to. For some students in today's fast-paced world, this may be the only time of the week where people actually focus on them and listen to what they are saying.
- *To improve students' listening ability*—When encouragements are given, students must listen to each and every comment carefully, so they will recognize when their idea has already been said. I impress upon the students that a person does not want to hear the same two comments about themselves repeated over and over, so if their idea for an encouragement has already been offered to the leader, they must try to think of a different one to give, or to modify an already-stated one.
- *To learn how to give compliments*—Students who are not used to this type of direct talk soon catch on to the art of encouragement by watching and listening to others in the group. For some, just making eye contact with the person to whom they are speaking is a challenge. When a student is the leader, he or she finds out how wonderful it feels to be encouraged, and is more apt to then encourage others.
- *To learn how to receive compliments*—Looking at the person who is speaking, and nodding or saying "thank you" when an encouragement is given, teaches students appropriate ways to respond when someone gives them a compliment.

(Note that although I use the word compliments interchangeably with encouragements here, students easily distinguish between this and the two different parts of the meeting)

difficult for anyone else to comment on the athletic ability of a student. Instead, many comments can focus on sports ability if each is specific in nature. For example:

- I notice that you're great at making 3-pointers in basketball
- I think you are good at passing the puck in floor hockey
- I like how you encourage your teammates when you play soccer
- I notice that you are getting better at doing cartwheels and handstands

Verbally share examples of encouragements that students suggest, or write them down on the board. After you have recorded several, check the encouragement chart to see if they match the criteria. You might want to throw in a comment about what someone is wearing or something they own (e.g., "I like your remote control car" or "I notice you have new jeans") so that you can reinforce the idea when checking the chart that comments about physical appearance or material possessions are not considered encouraging.

Practising Encouragement

It is important that students have a chance to practise encouraging statements. Explain to the students that it may feel awkward at first, but that with practice, they will get used to giving encouragements to each other. To get them to practise, you may wish to go quickly around the room verbally pairing students up. Or, if students are sitting beside each other, they can buddy with each other.

To help students practise encouraging statements, tell them to think about the other person and how that person is in the classroom, the gym, the playground, the music room or other areas around the school where students work or play. Ask:

- What is one thing you notice this person is good at?
- What do you notice this person is getting better at?
- What makes this person great to work with? ... to play with?

Remind students that encouragements must be positive. If students are having difficulty with encouraging statements, point to the three possible stems on the chart and say, "Use one of these to start your encouragement."

In addition to practising the words for encouragement, it is also a good idea to practise the actions. Explain to the students that they will need to:

- Make eye contact with the person to whom they are speaking
- Say their encouraging comment by stating the person's name, then the comment
- Say thank-you if they are receiving the encouragement

You may wish to model the above process with a volunteer from the class.

To decide which student will give an encouragement first, do a fun introductory activity to get them talking and feeling more at ease with each other. Giving them a way to decide who will go first also eliminates any argument that may occur. Some activities I have successfully used include telling the students:

- Start with the person whose birthday is closest to today
- Start with the person who lives closest to the school
- Start with the person who is the taller of the two
- Number yourselves one and two ... (two) starts

If students have to move to be near the person they are encouraging, make sure they move before they begin their encouragement. Indicate the end of the activity by clapping your hands, ringing a bell, or whatever method you normally use to bring the class back from a group activity. Afterward, ask the students, "How did you feel when you received the encouragement?" Guide discussion to help students verbalize the realization that encouragements make us feel good.

Once the students have had an opportunity to practise encouraging statements with a partner, tell them that each week, during the class meeting, they will be giving an encouragement to the leader. Suggest that they try to think of more than one thing they notice about a person, in case someone before them says the one thing they had planned on saying.

During the weeks preceding the first class meeting, you may feel the need to have the students practise giving and receiving an encouragement at least once more, pairing students up with new people. Often though, I find that doing it once is sufficient, as students soon see the process in action at meetings. Likewise, continually modeling your expectations by giving encouragements to your students helps reinforce the concept too.

It is also helpful at the beginning of each week during the year to put up the name of the student who will lead the meeting. Knowing who the leader will be that week gives the other students time to notice the person and to be thinking of possible encouragements. This is especially important for students who may not know the leader well.

Giving and receiving encouraging statements may initially be difficult for students, but they become very good at it with practice. They also become more comfortable making eye contact with the person with whom they are speaking.

Teaching the Problem-Solving Process

After your introduction on encouragement, spend the time scheduled for the class meeting the following week teaching your students about the process for problem solving. Since problem solving is such an important part of many existing curriculums, you may already have lessons introducing the process to students. If not, here is a suggested lesson sequence:

- Guide students into the idea of using a step-by-step process for solving problems by asking them about problems that have come up so far in the school year. You might begin with a question such as, "Does everyone always get along well with each other when they are at school?" or "What kinds of things make kids unhappy at school, and perhaps make them not want to come to school?" Lack of academic success may come up, and can be acknowledged as a factor, but the focus of the discussion which follows should be on the social and emotional aspects of school.
- Write ideas for problems they may have on the board as they are suggested. For example:
    - people being teased or called names
    - people bugging other people when they are trying to work
    - someone using someone else's calculator without permission
- Ask the students, "What usually happens in each of these instances? How does the problem get solved?" Students will provide many answers, most

of them focused on what the teacher normally does to try to stop the behavior.

- Ask, "What kinds of things do you try, yourself, to solve the problem?" Depending on their level of previous experience with cooperative learning, problem solving, classroom discussions about behavior, or other factors that would affect their growth in this area, any number of responses may be proposed. Most of the time, students will suggest one or several of the following, which I record on the chalkboard:

> How I Try To Solve Problems
> - tell the teacher
> - tell the person to stop
> - ignore the person
> - walk away

- Discuss each response and let the students tell you how successful they think each strategy usually is. Begin to establish the idea that there are definite strategies kids can try, and choices they can make, when trying to solve their own problems. Tell the students that you expect them to use strategies to try to solve problems on their own. However, explain that there are some problems that will need to be solved at class meetings.
- Introduce the idea of making choices from a number of possible solutions by using a realistic situation that is common in classrooms. One example I use that students often encounter is the problem with someone talking to you when you are trying to work. I say, "You have about five choices for what to do when someone is bugging you when you are supposed to be working. You can:
  - talk to them too
  - tell them be quiet
  - ignore them
  - put up your writing folder or another large item for privacy
  - move to another desk or table

Discuss each of the choices and elicit from the students possible consequences of each choice. Have them consider: Which ones might work? Which one is not a good choice? Why?

- Use an example of a problem the students might have in real life, such as arriving home after school and finding the door locked, to take them through the five steps that will be used in class meetings.
- Begin by gathering information to help clarify the problem by asking, "What are all the facts?" The students may tell you:
  - the door is locked
  - I have no key
  - my parents don't get home for one hour
- Ask students, "What information do you need?" Prompt them to ask questions to gather facts, such as:
  - is there another door I could try?
  - are any windows open?
  - is there another key hidden somewhere?
  - do I need to be in the house?
  - what is the weather like?

- Guide students into brainstorming possible solutions for solving the problem, using the new information gained from questioning. Write suggested solutions on the board. For example:
  - break a window
  - sit and wait
  - go to a neighbor's place
  - try another door
- Go over the possible consequences of each suggestion. Ask: What might happen if you break a window to get in? Is this a good solution to the problem? Why or why not? Is it reasonable? Do you have the resources to do it? etc. Ask the students to analyze each solution and discuss why they think the solution will or will not work.
- Have the students choose the solution they think will work the best by raising their hands to vote.
- Lead students in a brief discussion to determine what must be done to make the choice a reality. Making a plan to follow is an important part of following through on a decision.
- Explain that sometimes the solution you choose doesn't work. Ask students, "What do you think you do then?" Help them to see that they would go back to the solutions and try another one, or generate more solutions to choose from.
- Tell students that this is the basic process of solving problems that will be used in class meetings. The five steps include:
  - identifying the problem
  - brainstorming possible solutions
  - discussing solutions
  - choosing a solution
  - making a plan
- Hand out the sheet on the opposite page entitled "Steps in Solving Problems" that will be used to guide the class meeting leaders later on. Go over this with the students as a way of visually reviewing the steps in the process.
- Tell students to highlight the five steps and also to highlight the parts they will say when they are a leader. Instruct students to put the sheet into an appropriate folder or notebook.

Clarifying the Steps in the Problem-Solving Model

I've noticed that people get along when we have class meetings and after class meetings. I've also noticed that it helps people learn how to solve their everyday problems. Class meetings have solved many problems in the past, I guess. When I have a problem in the future, I am going to look back to class meetings. I also like class meetings because they are fun, because you learn in the process of solving problems, and I like solving problems.

Student, age 11

From class meetings I learn about what problems can happen between two people or more. It gives me a chance to help other people with their problems. The skills to solving problems is something so easy I'm pretty sure you could learn them, so try, and make your life a whole lot better!

Student, age 10

Steps In Solving Problems

1. IDENTIFY THE PROBLEM/GATHER FACTS AND FEELINGS

- Read out the problem and ask if it is still a problem.
  - a) If it isn't, ask, "What did you do to solve it?"
  - b) If it is still a problem, continue.
- Ask the person with the problem: "Can you tell us about the problem? What have you already done to solve this?"
- If another person is involved, ask "Is this true?"
- Ask "Does anyone have any questions?" (Keep asking for questions until problem is clear)
- Summarize: "It sounds like the problem is ..."
- Ask the person with the problem, "What do you think might solve this problem?"
- Ask the class, "Who thinks that this might work?"

If the majority of the students are satisfied with this solution, the problem is considered solved. If not, go on to #2.

2. BRAINSTORM POSSIBLE SOLUTIONS/CONSEQUENCES

- Ask "How do you think we can help _____?" or "What do you think might be a logical solution to this problem?"
- Secretary will record solutions generated.
- Go around the circle when asking for a response, taking hands that are up.
- People only get to speak once.
- Do not allow any discussion at this point—only solutions.

3. DISCUSS SOLUTIONS/CONSEQUENCES

- Say "Mrs./Mr. _____ will read all the suggestions."
- Ask people which suggestions might or might not work and why.
- When people seem to be saying the same thing, summarize, then ask for comments on other solutions.

4. CHOOSE A SOLUTION/CONSEQUENCE

- Students can vote only once. Remind them that a logical solution is one that they think would best help the person or solve the problem.
- Count hands to decide choice.

5. MAKE A PLAN

- If the choice involves a plan, figure out who will do what to make the solution happen.

A number of curriculums, particularly for subject areas such as Math and Social Studies, include the solving of problems as a skill to be mastered by students. Spending a certain number of weeks teaching students how to solve a problem, or involving them in problem-solving exercises certainly has merit. However, what better way to really internalize the process than by giving students 35 practices over the year based on content that involves them personally? This is the real value of using a formal process to solve problems in class meetings. Students will later tell you that they take what they learn about solving problems in meetings and are able to apply the process outside the classroom.

In order to run class meetings smoothly, you must, as the teacher, be clear on the steps involved in the problem-solving process. It is important to know when brainstorming solutions, for example, that evaluation or discussion of each suggestion is not appropriate. Meetings can easily get off track if students continually bring up issues or interject with ideas that muddy the proceedings. With your guidance, student leaders soon learn to respond to comments that are out of order with a gentle reminder of the step the group is now on. You will find that this eliminates many of the problems that plague meetings that do not have a formal method in place. Meetings can easily become gripe sessions unless certain conventions are followed.

Identifying the Problem

Though it sounds simple, identifying the problem is not an easy task. Sometimes what appears to be fairly straightforward can, after probing, actually be a whole different problem. For example, when hearing a student make the common accusation "Someone stole my pencil!" it might seem that someone taking the pencil is the cause. However, the real problem might be "I can't find my pencil." Identifying the wrong problem leads to coming up with the wrong solution. In this case, the solution to solving a problem where someone is stealing pencils (e.g., putting a video camera in the class) would be completely different from the solution for a person not being able to find their pencil (e.g., cleaning out your desk).

Often, the questioning that needs to be done is skipped over, and solutions are based on assumptions rather than fact. Gathering information about the problem is critical to generating good solutions. Putting this in the context of a class meeting:

- The leader reads out a problem and asks if it is still a problem. If it is not, the leader says, "What did you do to solve it?" Students need to hear affirmation of their own problem-solving abilities and note growth in their skills. Since this problem is considered solved, the leader goes directly to the next item in the box.
- If the student says it is still a problem, the leader asks the person to elaborate with, "Can you tell us about it?" The student then explains the problem.
- The leader then asks, "What have you already done to solve this?" It is important for the class to know what strategies have already been tried and been unsuccessful, as this information will affect the solutions they generate later on in the process.

Difficulties with students tattling on others will be reduced if the students are expected to give an account of how they have tried to solve their problems first. It is expected that they must try to solve their own problems in at least one or two different ways so that the classroom meeting becomes a last resort to common squabbles and day-to-day disagreements that happen as students live and work together in their classroom.

Dr. Dawn Benson, Director of Instruction, School District #83, Salmon Arm, BC

- If another person is named in the problem, the leader asks the person submitting the problem, "Is this true?" The wording here is very precise for a number of reasons:
  - The person who owns the problem is the one who put it into the box, not the person causing the problem. If the leader were instead to ask the perpetrator what they thought the problem was, the perpetrator would be taking over ownership of the problem.
  - When asked if this is true, the student can only respond with a "yes" or "no," but may give additional detail. This avoids defensive behavior and keeps the group focused on problem identification.
  - Only the person who has put the concern in the box and the person or people who are named can speak to the problem, no one else. This prevents tattling or ganging up on the person who may be causing the problem. The other students may ask questions only, but may not offer comment, in the next step of the process.
- The class now knows what the problem seems to be, and what the person supposedly causing it has admitted to. The students' job now is to ask questions until they have a clear picture of what is going on. The leader asks, "Does anyone have any questions?"
- Students (and adults) raise their hands to speak and wait until the leader calls upon them to pose a question. Students address the person to whom they wish to ask the question, and may speak to both parties involved. This is a critical phase, as the better the questions asked, the clearer the problem becomes. Groups who rush through this step often choose solutions that are less than satisfactory, and they soon learn to spend more time finding out all the facts, thoughts and feelings surrounding the problem.
- After the problem seems clear, the leader summarizes with, "It sounds like the problem is ... " Initially, when students start to lead meetings, you will need to raise your hand and tell the leader when to summarize, and guide them in doing this.
- The leader returns to the student who brought the problem up, and asks, "What do you think might solve the problem?" Sometimes, during the question phase, the student thinks of something that might work, and he or she offers it at this point.
- If this is the case, the leader asks the class, "Who thinks that this might work?" Hands are raised, and if a healthy majority of the students are satisfied with this solution, the problem is considered solved. If few hands are raised, or it seems to be evenly split, the leader goes on to the next step.

Brainstorming Possible Solutions

Now that the group has identified what the problem is, and has some information about it, the group can suggest possible solutions. As solutions are generated, you, as the secretary, record them on your tracking sheet. As with any brainstorming activity, evaluation of ideas is not allowed at this stage. Discussion of each suggestion takes place after students have completed the generation of ideas.

In the beginning, particularly with students inexperienced with class meetings, you may find students suggesting solutions that are quite unrelated to the problem, or that require the teacher to do the work of overseeing a consequence. As students adjust to the power they have in meetings, and the responsibility they have in determining what might be most helpful to their peers, they soon contribute ideas that will surprise you in their sensibility and effectiveness. Five to six suggestions is ideal, but there are sometimes more or less than this number given.

A note of caution—although you may clearly see what will work best, refrain from participating in this step. You want students to learn how to decide upon practical, workable solutions, and the best way to do that is to let them learn from experience what works and what does not. Have faith in your students, and watch them slowly improve in their ability to find excellent solutions to problems.

Discussing Solutions

To help students learn about the consequences of their decisions, they must have experience discussing what they think will or will not work to solve a problem and why. By the time a vote is called to choose a solution, students will have a clearer idea of what solutions might work best, if they have heard arguments for and against during this discussion portion of the meeting. The points shown on this page can be used to reinforce criteria for a good solution.

Criteria for a Good Solution

A good solution:
- Is one that will be most helpful to the person(s) involved, rather than being punishing.
- Is related to the problem in that it addresses the root of the problem.
- Is respectful to the parties involved, and not humiliating or embarrassing in any way.
- Ensures that the person responsible for causing the problem is the one that suffers the consequence or does the action decided upon to solve the problem—not the teacher or other members of the group.
- Is reasonable in its ability to be carried out in terms of time, place, personnel or resources.

To open discussion, the leader will ask you, the secretary, to read out the possible solutions. As you read out each solution, precede it with a number, so students begin to form a clear image of the various options. In some situations, you may wish to remind students of the criteria for a good solution.

After the solutions are read out, the leader takes hands, and students offer comments such as, "I think #3 will work because ..." or, conversely, "I don't think ... but ... will work because ..." To help guide the leader, suggest that if several statements have been made for or against a certain solution, that they should ask the group to comment on other solutions that have not had much discussion. Also, if it seems that enough discussion has taken place, and there is an obvious lean toward or away from numerous solutions, suggest to the leader that he or she call the vote for a solution.

Choosing a Solution

At this stage, the leader asks you to read out the solutions one more time. As the secretary, you read each solution and then count the hands that are raised for the different solutions. Continue in this fashion until all solutions have been read. Students can vote only once. Show students that their vote is valuable and necessary to the process. If you see you are missing votes (i.e., they don't add up to the total number of members), conduct the vote again. After the vote, tell the students which solution has been chosen.

I use voting with an obvious majority for deciding upon a solution. By obvious majority, I mean that it is clearly the choice of the bulk of the class. Any time this does not happen, it usually shows student dissatisfaction with the solutions suggested, indicating that no solution suggested will clearly work in their estimation. In this case, you have three options:

- Go with the slim majority—remind students that decisions only have to be lived with for one week before they are revisited
- Return to the solutions and suggest combining or modifying them to generate more possibilities—only if time allows
- Suggest that perhaps the class needs another week to think about solutions and defer the problem to the next meeting—then let them decide what to do

Some teachers conduct secret votes, where students cover their eyes when the vote is taken. I believe students should vote openly, and be proud of taking a stand for what they believe. You may notice students watching others, then deciding how they will vote. Discuss this with them, explaining that they need to listen to the discussion and decide for themselves what solution will work, not just go along with what their friends vote for. I tell students that it doesn't matter if they are the only one voting for a solution—their point of view will be respected by the group.

Making a Plan

If the choice for a solution requires a plan (e.g., a student must write an apology letter), determine when, where and how this will be done. The student leader is often able to lead this, but sometimes you will need to speak to organize this. Where possible, give the student choices (e. g., Would you like to write it out at noon today or tomorrow?). Once a decision has been made, no further discussion on the topic is allowed, and the leader proceeds to the next item in the box.

Introducing Suggestion-Making and Committee Work

A lot of the things that I do now in Leadership 12 class, I learned in class meetings. Teamwork. We had to work together to solve the problems that came up.

Emily, age 17

Class meetings are not only for problem solving, but are also an opportunity for students to suggest ideas for activities they would like to do. Once a suggestion has been accepted, a committee is usually formed to make plans and organize the event. As the year goes on, you will find your students putting less problems into the box and more suggestions for things the class would like to do together.

As a teacher, you will find that meeting with committees throughout the year allows the opportunity to spend quality time with a small group of students in an enjoyable setting. It is virtually impossible on a day-to-day basis to connect individually with each and every one of your students. Working with a small group of students on a committee, even if your input is only required during the initial phase of a project, allows you to interact with students on a more personal level, and provides new insights into the skills and abilities of your students. The responsibility for planning activities, such as having a costume contest for Hallowe'en or making containers to hold exchanged valentines, can easily be turned over to your students, making for an enjoyable opportunity to simply sit back and let someone else plan the lesson! Some of the specific benefits for students of working on committees are listed below.

Committees—Benefits for Students

- Build leadership skills
- Learn organizational skills
- Improve ability to speak in front of the group (reporting progress)
- Gain confidence in personal abilities
- Become responsible
- See results of initiatives
- Enjoy the camaraderie of working with peers in a self-directed activity
- Get to meet with the teacher in another setting
- Feel a sense of accomplishment
- Feel valued and appreciated by the class

At the time that you are familiarizing your students with what class meetings are all about, you will need to introduce the concepts of suggestion making and committee work. To do this, you may wish to try out the following lesson sequence:

- Tell your students that meetings are not only for solving problems that come up, but are also a time for giving their ideas for activities or projects they might like to do as a class.
- Share several examples of things students have suggested in the past. For example, in my class, these include:
    - having a potluck luncheon
    - exchanging valentines and making creative containers to hold them
    - raising funds to donate to needy families in the community
    - having a car wash to thank parents who drove us on a field trip
    - designating a day as a Wacky Hair Day

  Each of these types of suggested activities requires organization and planning, which then becomes the responsibility of a committee chosen during a class meeting.
- Explain to the students that although they will have the opportunity to make decisions and plans, suggestions must first be approved by you. Empowering students by giving them a voice and allowing them to make choices does not preclude you from having control over what goes on in

your classroom. On the contrary, students will respect and accept your viewpoints, along with those of their classmates, when an honest exchange of ideas has taken place. My favorite example is, "I don't do sleepovers (in the class)!" I tell students that they may have had teachers in other years who do sleepovers, but that this is not something I am willing to do. However, I add that there are many other ideas that I am very willing to listen to.

- Hand out the sheet entitled "Steps in Discussing Suggestions" provided on the following page and have students put this into their designated folder or notebook for such material.
- Go over the steps outlined on the sheet, with special reference to #3, which reminds the students that they need to make sure they have your approval before proceeding with a suggestion.
- Tell students that they will be deciding on how committee members are to be chosen. I explain to students that in the past, students have usually asked the person who put the suggestion in if they would like to be on the committee. Then, other members are chosen. I find four to be an ideal number for committees, so I tell them this at the start. Students will usually bring up the problem of how to decide on who should be on a committee, and will develop quite elaborate methods of being "fair." As a teacher, I love this, because it absolves me of the responsibility of making these kinds of decisions, which can sometimes be quite arbitrary. When the majority of the class has agreed to a certain procedure, they follow it without question. If it is a flawed process, they soon discover this, and they will bring it up again, as a problem, in the class meeting box.
- Explain to students that working on a committee involves time outside of class, and effort. Committee members must give up lunch hours sometimes, and must be willing to work from beginning to end on a project or plan.
- Take time to answer any questions students might have.

Once a suggestion is made, and students see how the process works during a meeting, they will soon be putting suggestions in the box, and need no further explanations or lessons about this aspect of meetings. If you find that no suggestions are being made, put one in yourself to "get the ball rolling." See Chapter 6 for detailed ideas involving both student and teacher-generated activities that often first appear as suggestions at a class meeting.

Teaching and Practising Circle Formation

A circle is essential to respectful meetings. Students sitting on chairs formalizes the meeting, and helps keep fidgeting to a minimum. In a circle, everyone can see each other, and there is a sense of equality. Everyone feels included and valued as a group member. However, forming a circle quickly and quietly must be taught and practised. The following is the sequence I use early in the year to teach this skill:

- Teach students how to clear the room and form a circle. Demonstrate how to carry their desk with both hands, tilting it back a little so items do not fall out. Go over where each set of desks will be placed around the outer edges of the room. Show them how to carry their chair with two hands, one on the back of the chair and the other under the seat. Tell students that their

My advice to teachers? Keep the circle formation for meetings. It shows respect for everyone.

Emily, age 17

Steps in Discussing Suggestions

1. Read out the suggestion.

2. Ask the person(s) to tell us more about the suggestion.

3. Ask Mrs./Mr. _____ to comment on whether or not this is an idea that we can go ahead and discuss.

4. If it is, ask the students for their opinions.

   • Has anyone ever taken part in this before? How did it work?

   • What do they like or dislike about the idea?

   • Do they think it is worthwhile?

   • What might be the benefits?

   • What might be the possible problems?

5. Summarize: "It sounds like..."

6. Ask for a show of hands of people who would like to do this.

7. Make a plan of action: "How will we go about doing this?"

   • Form a committee, if needed, to organize the activity.

   • Ask the person putting in the suggestion if they would like to work on the committee.

   • Choose a committee of two girls and two boys.

   • Set a meeting time when the committee can meet with Mrs./Mr. _____.

   • Tell the committee it is to report back next week.

desks will be moved out of the way first, then they are to return to pick up their chairs and then move to their assigned place in the circle.

- Assign each student a specific place to sit in the circle. This ensures a quick, orderly formation of the circle, as students keep the same place all year long, regardless of where they are currently sitting in the class. Minimize possible problems by considering the following factors when deciding the order students will sit in:
  - alternating boys/girls
  - mixing high-low-frequency contributors to discussions
  - separating disruptive students from each other
  - deciding where a classroom aide or interpreter will sit

Remember that you will not need a designated place in the circle, as, after the initial role of leader, you will be taking the chair of whichever student is leading the meeting that particular week, thus circulating around the circle as the year progresses.

- Explain that silence in the circle formation is critical to establish the tone of the meeting. This must be practised, and classes may need several tries before accomplishing a silent move. Once the class is able to move into the circle without speaking, a stopwatch may be used to begin working on the goal of forming the circle in under one minute. Achieving silence before doing any timing focuses the class on the importance of this aspect of circle formation.
- Teach students to use hand gestures to communicate during the silence. Once seated, they may have to motion for someone to move back or forward so that all members are visible.
- Designate a desk as the leader's desk. Choose whatever desk happens to be in the location you think will work to start the circle formation. Before forming the circle to begin each meeting, ask the student leader to put his or her desk to the side and move to the leader desk to begin looking at the contents of the class meeting box, while the rest of the class is forming the circle.
- Have the students practise forming a circle for a class meeting. At this stage, you will take the chair and desk of the leader for the practice. When everyone is seated and waiting, evaluate with the students how they did. If any students spoke or whispered, remind them of the importance of silence.
- Ask students to return the room to normal, without speaking.
- Discuss what happened once students have returned to their usual seating plan. Go over any reminders. Try it again. If the class is still not able to form the circle quickly and quietly, tell them they will have an opportunity to try again next week.

I liked how everyone moved so quietly and quickly. I liked how everyone sat back in their chairs so everyone could see everyone.

Student, age 9

By this point, you will probably find that the students will want to have a meeting, so will be motivated to correctly form the circle next time. If you insist on silence right from the start, and do not begin meetings until the class achieves this, you will be rewarded all year with quiet, efficient movement of furniture and people for meetings. If the students were successful the first time—a rare occurrence—encourage a job well done with a positive comment, and proceed with your first meeting.

Preparing Necessary Materials

A few items will need to be prepared in advance of the first meeting, and discussed with the students. These include the class meeting box, guide sheets for the leader, the secretary binder, and recording the weekly meeting on the class timetable.

The Class Meeting Box

The class meeting box is a central prop in the class meeting process, as it is the place where problems and suggestions are collected prior to the meeting, and one of the items that the leader will have in front of him/her at the meeting. The week before your first meeting, ask for two volunteers to prepare the class meeting box so it is ready for the following week's meeting. To prepare one:

- Provide a small box, such as a shoe box, with a lid that can be opened or removed. Cut a slot into the top, about 2" x 1/2", to allow for folded papers to be dropped into the box.
- Show the two volunteer students any materials available for them to use (e.g., construction paper, cloth, buttons, pipe cleaners, felt pens, glitter, etc.) to decorate the box.
- Explain to the students that they can cover the box and decorate it any way they wish, remembering that the lid must still open. Add that the words "Class Meeting Box" should be written on the box.
- Provide time in class, or during recess or lunch, for the students to get the box ready.

Once the box is ready, place the finished box on a counter, shelf or low cabinet where it can be easily accessed by the students. Inform the students that the box is now ready to be used. Point out that students may use any small scrap piece of paper to write down problems or suggestions that are going into the box. Remind them that they need to write down:

- Their name
- The date
- The problem or suggestion

Make sure that the students understand that before they put a problem in the box, they must:

- Try to solve a problem on their own first
- Understand that the purpose of the box is not to tattle on someone or to get a person into trouble
- Refrain from removing anything that is in the box—the box is only to be opened by the leader during the meeting
- Make sure the student's name and the date are written on the paper

Guide Sheets for the Leader

Make one copy of each of the following reproducible sheets, and laminate them if possible. These will serve to guide the leader during the meeting, and can be kept with the class meeting box.

- Class Meeting Agenda (found on page 21)
- Steps in Solving Problems (found on page 35)
- Steps in Discussing Suggestions (found on page 42)

The Secretary's Binder

As the secretary, I find it useful to keep track of weekly meeting business by using a small three-ring binder where I can record:

- The date
- The leader
- Problems/suggestions
- Solutions/plans
- Choices

The reproducible tracking sheet provided on the following page can be photocopied (about 35 copies), hole-punched, and placed in the secretary's binder, which should be labeled "Class Meetings."

Timetable

It is important to write "class meeting" on your weekly timetable. If possible, try to choose a period right before or right after a natural break in the day, such as recess or lunch. Preferable days for meetings are Wednesdays or Thursdays. Consistency is important, and avoiding Mondays and Fridays, typical holiday days, ensures that meetings will not be missed and will be held on a regular basis. Also, when meetings are held later in the week, it allows for more student interaction time so that problems and suggested activities can be discussed prior to the meeting, thus providing substance for meetings.

Monday	Tuesday	Wednesday	Thursday	Friday
bellwork ——————————————————————————————————————→				
sign ——→				
Student-of-the-week Rdg/Wrtg	Rdg/Wrtg * P.E.	Rdg/Wrtg	Rdg/Wrtg	Rdg/Wrtg ART
RECESS				
Spelling Math	Math Buddies	Math * P.E.	Class Meeting Math	French Math
LUNCH				
*Music	*Book Talk/ D.E.A.R.	French	*Music	Student-of-the-week Guest Rdg/Wrtg
S.S./S.C.	S.S./S.C.	S.S./S.C.	S.S./S.C.	* P.E.
Closing ——————————————————————————————————→				

Class Meeting

Date: _____   Leader: _____

Problem/Suggestion:

_____

_____

Solutions/Plans:

1. _____

2. _____

3. _____

4. _____

5. _____

Choice: _____

Problem/Suggestion:

_____

_____

Solutions/Plans:

1. _____

2. _____

3. _____

4. _____

5. _____

Choice: _____

4 Running Effective Meetings

As in any well-structured lesson, preparing for each part of the lesson is critical to success. Class meetings are no exception. For meetings to be effective, the aspects of each component must be clear in your mind, and any necessary materials must be available.

Establishing routines and expectations for behavior, clearly outlining the roles each member is to play at meetings, and organizing materials in advance will help meetings run more smoothly. When students know what is expected of them, and their roles in class meetings are clearly explained, they will feel comfortable entering into meetings and will be confident of their ability to succeed.

As you conduct meetings, you will develop your own style, modifying components as you go along. However, I have found that having somewhere to begin is helpful, and I therefore offer the following suggestions as a starting point in helping you run meetings effectively. Many of the sections below have already been touched on in previous chapters—the information here is intended to add to and clarify points about particular procedures or roles.

The Agenda

My class meetings always follow the same format, beginning with the Encouragement Circle, and if time, ending with Thank-you's and Compliments. The main part of the meetings always deals with problems and suggestions the students (or the teacher or adults working in the room) bring up—New Business—as well as previous problems and suggestions—Old Business. An agenda helps remind the students, especially the leader for each meeting, what the format is.

Determining the Agenda

Class meetings deal with both problems and suggestions, which students (or the teacher) have written down for the meeting. Teachers use a variety of methods to collect concerns or ideas that will determine the new business for meetings. Some I have seen in use are:

- List or chart posted on a bulletin board or wall
- Notebook or special book
- Box (or other container) with opening in lid

Class Meeting Agenda

- Open the meeting
- Encouragement Circle
- Old Business
- New Business
  - problems
  - suggestions
- Thank-you's and Compliments
- Close the meeting

I have personally tried the method of using a posted chart, but found it to be less than satisfactory. A posted agenda (or a book) gives students a chance to see the content of the next meeting, which can often cause problems—sometimes more serious than the original problem posted. When students see a problem written on a chart (or in a book), it can lead to arguments about what is written down, and can cause groups of students to take sides on issues before they are dealt with appropriately or respectfully in a meeting atmosphere.

Even if a discussion does not take place, when a student sees that he or she has been named in a problem, he or she may show animosity toward the other student, which can lead to increased problems between the two in the week leading up to the meeting. In younger students, I have found that it can lead to revengeful behaviors as well, wherein a student will see themselves named in a problem, then want to retaliate by writing up something about the other student.

Using a box, which cannot be opened until the meeting, eliminates many of these possible problems from occurring. I have found the box to be highly successful, and now use this method in my classroom.

Dealing with the Contents of the Class Meeting Box

Slips of paper are used for entries to be made into the box. Generally, there are three types of issues put into the box:

- A problem involving one or more people
- A problem or issue affecting the whole class
- A suggestion for an activity to do

In addition to the issue at hand, a name and date must appear on the paper. Just before the meeting begins, it is the job of the leader to sort out the contents of the box while the rest of the class is forming the circle, and separate the slips of paper into two piles—problems and suggestions—which will be dealt with in that order.

The order of the agenda is determined by the dates on the slips of paper, with the earliest dated problems being brought to the table first. If no date appears on a paper, it is put last in its pile, and is brought up after all dated entries.

If no name is on a problem or a suggestion in the box, it is not dealt with. Students need to take the responsibility of identifying themselves in relation to the problem so they can speak to the issue. In respect to whomever may be mentioned in a problem, no problem is read out without first identifying the person who put the problem in the box. This reduces the possibility of students putting things into the box just to tattle or to get someone into trouble. Once an issue is not discussed at a meeting because of the absence of a name, students catch on very quickly to this expectation, and realize the importance of taking ownership for problems.

Students are accountable for their actions when they must explain themselves to their peers. If one particular student is causing a problem, that student is named for two reasons:

- So he or she may have the opportunity to present his or her point of view
- So he or she can see how his or her peers view the misbehavior

In this way, students begin to develop an understanding that their behavior has an effect on others, and that they are accountable to the group for their actions. Realizing that peers do not approve of certain behaviors is a powerful agent for change.

Today in class meeting, I found out what it's like to be the keeper of the problem.

Student, age 11

No one can go into the class meeting box except the leader, at the time of the meeting. If a problem has been solved in the meantime, or students want to alter or rescind a suggestion, there is a time for this in the meeting when the leader asks, "Is this still a problem?" If it has been solved, there is no further discussion. Suggestions can be explained or elaborated upon when the student has the chance to speak about his or her ideas for the suggestion. Knowing that they are not allowed to retrieve papers once they have put them into the class meeting box, and that they will be questioned about the problem by the meeting leader, make students try to solve problems on their own before putting them into the box for the class to solve.

If there is nothing in the box, the meeting progresses as per usual, following all the steps. The only element missing will be New Business. The Encouragement Circle, where students focus comments on the student leader, still takes place. Old Business is reported on, and there are often committee reports during this time, as well as a revisitation of last week's problems, when you ask how things have gone. There will definitely be time for Thank-you's and Compliments on such a day. Students enjoy having an empty box at times so they can finally pass on their compliments to the rest of the group, as there often is not time for Thank-you's and Compliments at the end of meetings.

The Physical Setting

Circles, an important part of many cultures' rituals and beliefs, signify cohesiveness and can have a magic all their own. Using a circle to hold meetings ensures equality of members, with no one person at the "head." Even the leader, though seated at a desk, is at the same level as the rest of the members of the group. The simple act of moving their desks out of the way, and bringing their chairs into the center of the room to form a circle gives students the message: "Something important is happening here."

Chairs and Desks

I have tried having meetings with students sitting on the floor, rather than using their chairs, but find students to be fidgety, less focused, and having a harder time concentrating on the proceedings. Sitting on chairs dignifies the meeting, making it a little more formal. When establishing the overall expectations for meetings, remind students to keep their feet still.

I recommend using a student desk for the leader to put the class meeting box and guideline papers on. In my class, we just use whatever desk happens to be in the spot we form the circle from each week. Sometimes, additional furniture needs to be moved out of the way before you call the class to a meeting. In my present room, we move a large table and the overhead projector out of the way before moving into the circle.

When students come to the circle and sit down in their chairs, they are required to use hand gestures to motion people to move back until each member is sure he or she can see every other member. Students catch on to this very quickly, and take no time at all to ensure clear visibility of members. When the leader sees that all gesturing has stopped, and that everyone's eyes are on him or her, he or she calls the meeting to order.

In a circle, it helps you learn, because everyone is quiet and only one person speaks.

Student, age 11

Forming the Circle

Go slowly when practising the circle formation process. You want to establish a respectful tone right from the start, so insist on silence and keep practising until you achieve it. Talk to the students about respecting the classes around you (and perhaps below you) by moving their desks and chairs quietly. Since this will be a weekly event, it is important to be able to do it quickly and without fuss. As well, silence ensures that everyone is concentrating on the task at hand, reducing the possibility of accidents or mishaps.

Take time to establish this expectation right at the start, practise it, and compliment a job well done. If you are firm about these expectations, clearing your classroom and forming a circle of chairs will not be a formidable task, but a painless routine. Once students can form the circle quietly, use a stopwatch to time how long it takes and strive for about a minute or less (our record this year was 37 seconds). Some classes achieve this goal very quickly, while others will take more practice. After the routine is established, abolish the stopwatch.

Placement in the Circle

When students sit in the same location in the circle all year, this helps the circle to be formed quickly. Factors to consider in deciding on this arrangement, and ideas for teaching the formation of a circle, are provided in Chapter 3.

Having the teacher sit in the chair of the student leading the meeting changes the position of the teacher in the circle each week. This gives all students the opportunity, at some time during the year, to be seated next to the teacher. Since the teacher is the secretary, this allows students to look on to see what the secretary is writing during meetings, reinforcing for them the steps in conducting meetings.

Time Management

In grades four to six, one 40-minute period per week is a good amount of time for a class meeting. It is important to put it on the schedule, and to have a meeting every week, even if there are no papers in the meeting box. As suggested earlier, meetings are best scheduled around natural breaks such as recess or lunch—either right after a break or backing onto a break. The success of the latter time slot depends upon how reliable you are, as the teacher, in stopping your lessons to begin meetings. Personally, I find that starting right after a break, like recess, works best for consistency. Whatever time of day you hold your meeting, stick to your timeline of one period. Items not dealt with are held over to the following meeting.

The Value of Scheduling Time

Forty minutes for a class meeting is suggested for students in grades four to six as this is the typical length of a class period for these grade levels. Primary classes may hold shorter meetings, and secondary classes longer ones. However, sticking to a finite time period is critical for two reasons:

- Meetings can drag on when there are a lot of entries in the box
- Students become efficient with the problem-solving process when they know they have a limited time

Problems are best discussed with calm minds. If meetings are spontaneously called, instead of scheduled, students may not have time to "cool off" or to think about the problem in a rational way. Many times, a student will put a problem in the box, but during the time leading up to the meeting, resolves it on his or her own.

Scheduling meetings also shows students you value them, and ensures that meetings will not be missed. Remember that meetings serve many purposes, only one of them being the resolution of problems.

Sticking to a Schedule

I have found a timer helpful in sticking to a schedule. I use the type normally found in kitchens, where after the desired number of dialed minutes has elapsed, a bell dings. It is a good idea to use some sort of timer when you first start conducting meetings, as it is very easy for meetings to run on. This is because when students are first given the opportunity to take part in meetings, many concerns are brought up, making the agenda long. Also, group problem solving is not easy, and takes much longer than individual problem solving. Although time must be taken to fully discuss issues, you will find that as you and your students become more experienced, you will summarize items earlier in a discussion, and use other strategies that help move decisions along more quickly.

Initially, however, you may find that you don't accomplish much at meetings in terms of getting through all the slips of paper in the box. This is normal as you and your class are becoming familiar with the process. Problems or suggestions that have not been brought up for discussion due to a lack of time are simply put back into the box to be solved or discussed the following week. I find that this normally does not present a problem, as you do get "caught up" at future meetings. Students begin to solve their own problems more easily as well, so when the paper is read out the following week, the student has often already found a solution, thereby eliminating the need to discuss it at the meeting.

If there are a number of problems left that have not been discussed, I may ask the leader to please read out the problems and simply ask the individuals if there is still a problem. Some will have been resolved, and can be thrown out, while others will be put back into the box for the next meeting. In this case, if it is still a problem, sometimes hearing it read aloud will prompt the people involved to find a solution during the week, and it will also have been resolved by the next meeting.

Expectations for Class Meetings

Classroom norms and expectations are established through the meeting format and suddenly instead of the class "against" the teacher, with the teacher trying to impose his or her will on the class, it becomes the class "with" the teacher, focusing on "what's helpful or needed here?" The focus becomes a shared responsibility for what happens in the class. I've seen primary children as young as grade one and two taking turns chairing such meetings with the teacher joining the circle as part of the group.

Dr. Dawn Benson, Director of Instructor,
School District #83, Salmon Arm, BC

There are a few expectations that are important for students to understand and abide by in order for meetings to run smoothly and be effective. Some may be established at the start, while others can be dealt with in a "teachable moment" as they arise.

Setting the Tone for Meetings

It is important that students accept the idea that class meetings are not about punishment or revenge, but rather, are to be supportive and helpful in nature. As Dr. Benson explains earlier, the focus is on what the class can do to help each other, and the ownership as a class of problems and their solutions or consequences. Students learn very quickly that tattling or revengeful behavior (trying to get back at someone) is not accepted.

A respectful tone is established right from the start with the first question from the leader, "Can you tell us what you have done to solve the problem?" If the student says he or she has not done anything, the leader suggests that the student first try to solve the problem on his or her own before bringing it to the meeting. If the student says he or she has done something to solve it, it becomes obvious if he or she is being truthful, as the person named in the problem gets to speak next, and will say whether or not this is true.

Most importantly, the attitude students bring to class meetings is one which you, as the teacher, have promoted. In preparing for meetings, you will need to invite students to explore questions such as, "What if someone is constantly bugging another student—what might be the reason for that behavior? How do you think we can best help that person?" Establish the idea that misbehavior is a call for help, and that class meetings are about finding ways to help.

To prevent meetings from turning into gripe sessions or an avenue for tattling, be clear on one very important step in the process—in a problem involving two people, the only people who can talk about the problem are the person who put it in the box and the person who is named in the problem. That is the end of presenting the problem. No one else is allowed to jump in and tell about their particular dealings with the named person, or previous things that have happened, or corroborate with either person. Only questions may then be asked by the group to help clarify the problem. Once the situation is clear, the leader summarizes the problem, and the solution-finding phase begins.

Expectations for Circle Behavior

After successfully forming the circle for the first time, (silently and quickly), and before beginning the meeting, speak to the class about your expectations for behavior in the circle environment. The following are my expectations:

- Do not bring anything to the circle
- Sit still during the meeting with feet on the floor
- Raise your hand to speak during the meeting
- Wait to be called upon by the leader
- Speak one person at a time
- Look at the person who is speaking
- Keep hands down when people are speaking

Remind students that they must first attempt to solve problems on their own, two or three times, before putting them in the box. This eliminates the trivial problems that students are expected to solve themselves.

Encouraging the Leader

All students are expected to encourage the leader of the meeting. Although they may pass the first time people are commenting around the circle, they must provide a comment when their turn comes up again.

Some students are not organized enough to prepare themselves for the meetings, even when they know who the leader will be, or are less able to generate encouraging comments until they have more practice with it. I have only once had a problem with a student not having an encouragement ready. After this happened week after week, I asked the student to take the class list home and to write out one positive thing the person noticed about each student in the class. The list was kept in a notebook, and the student was then able to look at this list each week before coming to the meeting, thereby being prepared to share the encouragement.

Having to make an encouraging comment to the leader guarantees that every single member of the class speaks at the meeting. Participation by way of speaking, in the rest of the meeting, is optional, so Encouragement Circle is the only time each student must participate. As with anything, practice makes perfect. Having to speak at least once each week provides the less able students with the practice they need to improve their confidence level at meetings, contributing to their eventual love of meetings and improved ability to speak in front of a large group. It is important to remember that while encouraging the leader is mandatory, giving a thank-you or compliment at the end of a meeting is totally optional.

Generating Helpful Solutions

There must be an understanding that all members of the circle are to be treated with equal respect when they offer a comment or when they are the subject of others' comments. When students generate solutions to problems, or are proposing consequences for misbehaviors, they must be respectful of the people involved in the problem. I remind students that solutions or consequences must not be embarrassing to people or cause them to feel badly about themselves.

Helpful solutions are ones that are directly related to the problem. Initially, inexperience with the power of deciding consequences for their peers may cause some students to suggest solutions where the student must do something that is totally unrelated to the misbehavior. As students gain experience, and improve in their discussions of what might work and what might not, they soon begin to see which solutions are truly helpful, and they start to generate excellent ideas for resolving issues.

As well, students begin to see that the person responsible for carrying out the solution must be the person who has caused the problem. For example, it is not respectful to the teacher (or anyone else in the class) for students to decide that someone else must keep track of certain behaviors or conduct some elaborate scheme to get a student to behave, while the student himself or herself is doing nothing toward the solution. Again, with experience, the class will soon come up with ideas where the person with the misbehavior is the one who suffers the consequence for his or her actions, or is the one responsible for meeting the requirements for the solution, and not someone else.

Respecting the time involved and the reasonableness of a consequence or solution is also important. Students learn that certain ideas, while interesting, are not possible in the school setting, for one reason or another.

Dealing with Inappropriate Suggestions

Dealing with inappropriate suggestions is handled by having the leader ask you if the class can go ahead and discuss the suggestion that has been read out. If it is something you cannot agree to, you simply veto it. Students understand that although there are many things they do have a say in, some things, such as how much physical education is in their curriculum, are not up for negotiation.

Sometimes an explanation may be given for vetoing a proposal, but it is not always necessary. I find that when students see that you truly stand behind your belief in class meetings, and allow them to discuss and decide upon issues most of the time, they are very accepting of your viewpoint when you say you are not willing to discuss an idea that has been suggested.

Misbehavior during Meetings

If a student does not follow the "rules" laid out regarding meetings, indicate to the student leader (e.g., nod of your head, raised eyebrows, etc.) that he or she must deal with the behavior. If the student leading the meeting does not deal with the misbehavior, raise your hand and suggest to the leader that he or she remind the person of the meeting expectations. Help the leader to verbalize this, if needed.

If the behavior continues, raise your hand so the leader calls upon you. Remind the misbehaving student that to be part of the meeting, he or she must comply with expected behavior. In extreme cases, if the student chooses to continue misbehaving, I would raise my hand again to have the floor, and I would tell the student to leave the meeting for a "time out." It is then important to follow up after the meeting with whatever system you use for a time-out situation.

Recurring Problems with One Student

Sometimes there is one student in the class who seems to be blamed, rightly or wrongly, for recurring misbehavior. This is usually a student who has a great deal of difficulty emotionally or socially, and is a student you need to work with on an individual basis. If the student is not already on a behavior contract, this may be in order. Or, you may personally have to meet with the student to discuss the misbehavior, and formulate a plan for improvement.

I have experienced two cases of this, and in each case the student was already on a behavior plan or contract. After the same name came up a few times in class meetings, I explained to the class that this student and I had made up a plan to help him/her be successful in our class, and that in future they were to come directly to me if there were any difficulties, rather than bringing it up at meetings. Once your class understands that issues with this one student are being dealt with, the need for the help of the whole class in solving the problem is eliminated.

Duties of Group Members

Each participant in a class meeting, including the teacher, must adhere to certain norms to make the meeting run smoothly. Some of these were discussed in the previous section, but are summarized again below.

Duties of Group Members

- Move to circle quietly
- Wait for leader to call meeting to order
- Give an encouragement to the leader
- Listen respectfully
- Participate in discussion
- Raise hand to speak
- Wait to be called upon
- Stay on task
- Sit still
- Make eye contact with the speaker
- Ask questions to clarify issues at appropriate times
- Give a thank-you or a compliment (optional)

Duties of the Secretary

As with any type of group that meets on a regular basis, some accounting of what takes place at the meeting is necessary. As discussed earlier, a small binder for the secretary full of tracking sheets (see the reproducible page on page 46) suffices quite nicely.

For many years, I had students take on the secretary role at meetings, but found that much time was spent helping to record ideas, taking away from the business of the meeting. Students take a long time to record as they handwrite slowly, and this can hold up the meeting. The teacher can do this job efficiently.

Decisions from each meeting are kept track of and serve to guide the Old Business portion of the subsequent meeting. A record of what was discussed and decided upon gives value to the proceedings and provides good modeling for the students in how to conduct effective meetings. It sometimes also proves useful to go back into the binder to look at solutions that were chosen for a similar problem to one being discussed, as similarities among certain types of problems exist. In this way, students learn that previous solutions that were generated might also be applicable to new situations.

The secretary's major job is to write down problems and suggestions that are discussed at meetings. There are also three times during the meeting when you, as the secretary, will "have the floor" to direct the meeting proceedings. This occurs:

- During Old Business
- During the discussion of solutions
- Before voting

Our class meeting is not that different from our executive that we have at a kid's group.

Student, age 10

Duties of the Secretary during Old Business

The teacher plays an important role in guiding reflection on decisions made in previous meetings and redirecting solutions that need to be revisited. When the leader calls on you to report on Old Business:

- Say, "Thank you, (leader's name). We last met on (date) and (name) was our leader. We had (number) problems/suggestions that day."
- Read out each problem and the decision that was reached by the class. Afterward, ask involved students, "(Name), how did things go this week?"
- Revisit a solution if it has not worked. At this point, the student leader takes over, following the usual process for solving problems, with a new solution being decided upon to try for the next week.
- Ask any committees that need to report to do so.
- Say at the end, "And that's all for Old Business, (leader's name)." The student leader then takes over the meeting once again.

Duties of the Secretary during the Discussion of Solutions

There are a few occasions when the secretary assists during the discussion of solutions. You will need to:

- Read out the list of ideas generated for a problem
- Remind students that they are trying to choose a solution that they think will be most helpful
- Suggest that students consider the criteria for a good solution (see page 38 for more on this).

Duties of the Secretary before Voting

Just before a vote is to take place, the leader will ask the secretary to read out the suggested solutions or ideas. Your job at this point is to:

- Record the results of the vote and which solution or idea was chosen
- Suggest to the class that they may wish to modify or synthesize solutions in some way, or generate new ones, to find one that is satisfactory, in the event where a consensus or a healthy majority vote has not been reached
- Tell students to think about the possible solutions or ideas for a problem during the week if time has run out, and remind them that it will be brought up again next week

Duties of the Leader

For the first few meetings, you, the teacher, will be the meeting leader, and will model the duties of the leader for your students. After about the second meeting, if you think there has been enough material at meetings for the class to run through most aspects of a "normal" meeting and things have gone well, ask the class if anyone feels ready to lead a meeting.

Begin with those who ask first. Put their names on a list, then simply ask students to add their names to the list as needed during the year. You will find that the job of leader is less daunting if students can be the leader when they are personally ready. For some, this will be right away, while others will enjoy having twenty or more meetings as a participating member to become familiar with the process, before they volunteer to be the leader. When it gets down to the last few meetings in late May and early June, you may have to inform the few that are left that they will lead the meeting the next week or the following week.

On one occasion I had a student who was still very reticent about being the leader when everyone in the class had had a turn, and it came time for the last student to be the leader. I asked if he would perhaps like to have a friend sit beside him at the meeting to help him if needed. He agreed, and went into the meeting quite happily. As it turned out, after hearing the encouragements from his peers, he felt so good about himself that he was able to confidently lead the meeting without any assistance from his "helper" friend.

Class meetings really "kick into gear" when the students start to lead the meetings. There is a noticeable difference in the attitude of all students, and a respect for the talents of the student leader. As one student wrote: *I liked the class meeting today. John did a very good job, especially being the first in the class to be a leader of a class meeting. I would have been very nervous, but John wasn't that nervous. It was fun today.*

The designated student leader has a number of duties that he or she must perform, both before and during the meeting. These are outlined below.

Duties of the Leader before the Meeting

- Put his or her desk against the wall
- Go and get the class meeting box and accompanying guideline papers and sit at the desk designated as the leader's desk
- Dump out the papers in the box, read them and separate them into piles for both problems and suggestions, while the class is forming the circle
- Go get his or her own chair, and place it in the circle in the place he or she would normally sit (this is where the teacher [secretary] will sit that day)
- Return to the leader desk to wait until the class is settled and ready to begin
- Use any extra time to preview box contents

Duties of the Leader during the Meeting

- Keep meetings running smoothly
- Open and close the meeting
- Follow the order of steps for class meetings
- Follow the steps for solving problems
- Follow the steps for discussing suggestions
- Make eye contact with each person speaking
- Participate as any other member
- Keep discussion on topic
- Let students know if they are out of order
- Ask questions and help clarify or restate problems or ideas
- Summarize decisions or ideas
- Speak loudly and clearly

Clarifying the Role of the Teacher

Keeping the meeting running smoothly and staying on track is the job of the student leader. However, as the teacher, you will fulfill many other important roles, including:

- *Leader*—modeling the class meeting process and expectations for behavior at meetings during the first few meetings
- *Group member*—participating as a member in the proceedings of the meeting
- *Secretary*—making sure that meeting business is recorded at each meeting
- *Coach and facilitator*—helping students become successful as meeting participants and leaders

The Teacher as Class Meeting Leader

During the time when you are modeling the process of being a meeting leader, students are expected to be observers, listening to the proceedings and learning how to take part in them. When conducting the first few meetings, you are training the students to eventually facilitate meetings. In the first few meetings, while you are following the agenda and running the meeting, stop and explain to students what you are doing when you use techniques that guide the discussion. For example, in the following circumstances, you might say:

- Summarizing—"One job of the leader is to summarize the discussion. I will summarize what I think I have just heard. It sounds like the problem is ..."
- Keeping meetings running smoothly—"We have heard several comments about solutions 2 and 3. Does anyone have anything to say about solutions 1 or 4?"
- Reminding students they are out of order —"(Name) is out of order discussing this. It is time now for brainstorming solutions, not discussing them, so I am going to remind him of this."
- Reminding students of expected behaviors—"As the leader, I am now going to remind (name) not to keep a hand in the air when someone is speaking."

The Teacher as Group Member and Secretary

Once student leaders take over, you become a member of the group. This, of course, means following the same expectations as that of any other group member. For example:

- Raise your hand to speak
- Encourage the leader
- Listen respectfully
- Look at the person who is speaking

Due to your special role as secretary and your inherent role as the teacher, there are times during the meeting when you will not participate in the same manner as the students. To give the students ownership of the problem-solving process, ensure that solutions are generated by them and refrain from making suggestions during this stage of the process. The students need to feel that they are collectively making decisions, which helps them feel ownership for

I would tell the teacher that if you do class meetings people won't always be coming to you with their problems and they will learn to solve their own problems. I would also tell the teacher that you should have class meetings so you won't be planning things yourself.

Student, age 9

solutions agreed upon. Having said this, it is important to ask questions or make comments which you feel are pertinent or will help guide or redirect the discussion. This is a learning process for the students.

Sometimes you may not be sure which role you should be fulfilling. A good rule of thumb for distinguishing between the roles of group member and secretary is offered on this page.

The Teacher as Coach and Facilitator

Sometimes, when there is a pause in the proceedings, it is hard not to jump right in and tell the leader what to do. A guideline to remember is to remain quiet and give the student leader time to figure it out for himself or herself. In the first few months of class meetings, you may wish to point out the agenda sheet to remind the leader where to go next if he or she seems to be stuck. However, it is essential that you refrain from interrupting, from speaking out of turn, or taking over the leadership of meetings. If you think it is important to say something to help the leader be more successful, put your hand up and wait until you are acknowledged before you speak.

Early in the year, the students sometimes rush the questioning phase of gathering information about the problem, and go right into brainstorming solutions before they have correctly identified the problem. This can lead to choosing a poor solution, or one that you know will be ineffective or even unacceptable to the group. Instead of jumping in and "rescuing" the class, allow the students to proceed, as they will learn from the experience. Only by trial and error will the students begin to see which consequences or solutions are helpful and effective, and which are not. If students show dissatisfaction with a solution they have chosen, remind them that they only have to live with their choice for one week, and that it will be revisited the following week.

As leaders become familiar with running meetings, you can help them use the more advanced skills of reframing, summarizing and clarifying. If a meeting becomes a little unruly, and the leader is not dealing with it, you might raise your hand and suggest to the leader that he or she needs to call the group to order.

The following are some tips for being an effective class meeting facilitator:

- Model respectful behavior yourself
- Create a positive classroom environment
- Do not dominate meetings
- Refrain from making suggestions or generating solutions
- Have faith in the creative problem-solving process
- Trust the ability of your students to lead meetings, participate in discussions, choose solutions and make decisions that will affect the classroom

Summarizing the Duties of the Teacher

Given the variety of roles that the teacher plays in the class meeting process, the duties of the teacher are varied. The following chart summarizes the duties of the teacher both before and during the meeting.

Duties of the Teacher before the Meeting

- Get the secretary binder and a pen ready
- Ask the student leader to move his/her desk and prepare for the meeting
- Tell the students to get ready for the class meeting by having everything off their desks, and nothing on the floor
- Say, "You may move into Class Meeting," once the class is silent
- Sit in the chair in the circle normally used by the student leading the meeting, and wait for the student leader to call the meeting to order

Duties of the Teacher during the Meeting

- Participate as any other member of the group, raising a hand to speak
- Fill the secretary role
- Offer information only when needed. For example:
  - dates of upcoming events that may affect a planned activity
  - staff or school philosophy on an issue
  - factors that may be important to a decision and that students would not be aware of
  - information about something that the staff has planned that would impact on the discussion at hand
- Provide guidance to the leader, if necessary
- Make comments only when deemed necessary to keep the tone positive and helpful—for example, reminding students that the consequence or solution to a problem is one which will be most helpful to the student and is not a punishment

5 Creating a Respectful Classroom Environment

Classrooms built on the philosophy of belonging have caring, safe environments where children support and help each other. Such a philosophy promotes an "I can" attitude in all children. When children feel they belong, they feel safe and secure and good about themselves. As a result, they become tolerant of others, more accepting and forgiving.

Faye Brownlie and Judith King, authors of
Learning in Safe Schools

Academics are just part of what goes on in a classroom. The way the students feel about coming to school, how well they get along with their classmates, how accepted they feel, how much ownership they have toward their learning and how well they accept responsibility for their actions has a direct effect on their level of success as students. The climate of the classroom, in fact, has a great deal to do with academic achievement.

Class meetings are most successful in classrooms having a warm, caring, supportive environment. In these classrooms, students:

- Feel comfortable to learn
- Feel safe to share their ideas
- Feel free to ask questions and take risks
- Are supportive of each other
- Work together cooperatively
- Encourage each other
- Assume responsibility for their learning and behavior
- Are allowed to make decisions

Class meetings will go a long way toward creating such an environment in your classroom on their own, but when coupled with other strategies and activities can be even more effective. Modeling of respectful behavior by the teacher will greatly enhance the students' ability to do the same. Similarly, providing specific activities that promote a respectful classroom environment will enhance students' success at school.

This chapter provides ideas for activities that help to build and strengthen a positive affective environment in your classroom. These activities encourage students to develop a better awareness:

- Of self
- Of others
- Of themselves as members of a group

Building Self-Concept

A wealth of resources featuring activities that boost student self-esteem is available to teachers today. Books on cooperative learning have excellent ideas. Though they may seem to be just for "fun," these activities play a critical role in helping students learn more about themselves, thereby creating a climate that both accepts and respects individual differences in the classroom. The following are a few of my favorites.

Personality Packs

Though most commonly used to describe the main character in a book or the subject of a biography or an autobiography, character bags or boxes are also an interesting way for the students and the teacher to share their personalities, hobbies and interests. This activity serves to:

- Help the class get to know each other during the first few days of school
- Provide a forum for practising public-speaking skills
- Give students practice in making brief notes on a speaker
- Encourage active listening and questioning
- Model the feedback process of giving two compliments and a wish

Materials

- Paper bag
- Five items from home

Directions

- Bring in a small brown paper bag (Personality Pack) on the first or second day of school with five items from home. Instruct the students to write your name in their notebooks, underline it, and draw five dashes beneath it, ready for notes.
- Take out one item at a time, telling how it represents something about you. Help students to develop concise notemaking by condensing the information into a couple of words, and writing them on the board for students to copy. For example:
  - you say: "This miniature house represents my hobby of collecting little houses from the places I travel. I like to buy a souvenir, but often have no room in my luggage to carry large items, so I collect miniatures."
  - you write: collects miniature houses.
- Tell students that they are to bring in a Personality Pack to be shared with the class, and ask for five volunteers to begin the next day.
- Go over criteria for presenting, such as:
  - loud, clear voice
  - eye contact with audience
  - good expression
- Have five students a day share with the rest of the students, following the same format for notetaking as they did for your presentation.
- Invite two compliments and one wish from the class after each presentation.
- Leave the items on display for the day, then have students take them home.
- Review each day before the next five presenters begin by "quizzing" the class on previous presenters (e.g., Who collects houses and likes to ski?)

Sample Quiz Statements

1. She collects dolphins and likes dancing
2. He likes Lego and Halloween
3. A snowboarder who likes to draw
4. She likes TY's and silver jewellery
5. A pin collector who likes diving
6. He's a reader who collects Millennium coins
7. A ringette player who collects elephants
8. A skateboarder who loves to draw
9. He builds models and hunts with his Dad
10. He's a hockey player who likes to build with Lego
11. Collects miniature houses and skis
12. A skater who likes to watch movies
13. He collects Hotwheels and likes computer games
14. She's in 4-H and likes doing puzzles
15. A reader who loves all kinds of sports

- Consider, after all students have shared, having a Personalities Quiz, where students must identify the person being described. I encourage students to "study" for this test from their notes and give prizes for students achieving a perfect score.

Silent Messages

This activity is best done when students know each other, and it can take place at intervals throughout the year. It is a very encouraging activity, immediately boosting one's self-esteem.

Materials

- A pile of reusable paper, cut into note-size pieces (e.g., 2" x 6")

Directions

- Have monitors place a pile of papers on each student's or each group's desks, as well as yours.
- Tell the students that they will have the opportunity to write a message to everyone in the class. Explain the "rules":
  - messages must be positive
  - there must be a message, not just "hi"
  - students must sign their names
  - there is absolutely no talking
  - there is no running
  - students must try to write to as many class members as they can
  - there is a 10-minute time line
- Tell students that they will accomplish writing to more people if they write a few messages before getting up to deliver them.
- Instruct students to put delivered messages on the top-right corner of desks, so as not to interfere with the students writing messages.
- Explain to students that to maximize writing time, they are not to read any messages until the activity is complete.
- Tell students to try to write to everyone in the class.
- Remind students to sign their names to each message.
- Be firm about no talking, to ensure the success of this activity this time and in the future. Tell students that if anyone speaks, or whispers, you will stop the activity.
- Set the timer for ten minutes, and say, "You may begin."
- Consider focusing your writing efforts on students who you think may not get many messages.
- Say "stop" after ten minutes. Have the students deliver any messages they haven't yet delivered, then allow time for students to sit quietly and read their messages. There is usually silence, as students digest the contents of the messages.
- Process the activity with the students. For example: Did they enjoy it? How did they feel when they read their messages? Ask how many would like to do it again sometime. I normally have silent messages every two months or so. The students will ask for the activity if it has been awhile since the last time. Most enjoy it.
- Suggest to the students that they keep their silent messages for future use. Tell them they can staple their messages together, and keep them in their

Samples of Silent Messages from the Teacher

- Allison, thanks for helping out so much in the class. You really make my job easier!
- Tom, you are doing a great job with your little buddy. He wants to be just like you!
- Em, your French speaking is *formidable. Bravo!*
- Jenny, great performance yesterday. You wowed the audience!
- David, it's so great having you in this class. You get along well with everyone!

folder, so they can read them on days when things might not be going so well, and they need a little pick-me-up. Explain that the messages could become part of a "Feel Good File"—a collection of things that make us feel good about ourselves.

"Me" Mandala

Mandalas, found in various forms in ancient civilizations, provide one of the best strategies for bringing both "sides" of the brain into play—the linear, sequential skills, as well as the holistic, creative capabilities—and offer an excellent tool to use to address the needs of the visual learner.

Mandalas are great for making notes on any topic that has categories or sections in it, and can be adapted in size and content to suit a wide variety of purposes. In this activity, the students use a mandala to represent different aspects of themselves. Mandalas can also be used for other purposes, such as telling about a main character in a novel or organizing research notes.

With younger students, you may wish to start with three or four sections. The size I most commonly seem to use for this activity is six sections. This size can be done on 8 1/2" x 11" paper, and can also be blown up onto 11" x 17" paper on a copy machine. There must be enough room for students to be able to record information, so take into consideration the size of their writing and the amount of information, when deciding upon the number of spokes you will use.

When introducing any new strategy to students, I like to begin with something they are familiar with to model the process. Knowing the content for the "Me" mandala so well—information about themselves—students are able to focus on the criteria for creating a mandala, and do not need to worry so much about what they will write in the sections requiring information.

Materials

- Mandala for each child (photocopy one shown opposite onto 11" x 17" paper)
- Sample(s) of mandala(s) drawn on board or on an overhead
- Camera (optional)
- Criteria sheet (see page 66)
- Self-evaluation sheet (see page 82 in Chapter 6)

Directions

- Take a photograph of each student during the first week of school. Get double copies made—one for the mandala, and one for the cover of their learning journal (explained in this chapter). Alternatively, you may wish to ask the students to bring in photos of themselves from home or simply have them print their name in the center of the circle.
- Share with students the criteria for a mandala shown on page 66. As you go over each section, build student understanding by illustrating each point on a mandala about you on the blackboard or an overhead projector.
- Show students the self-evaluation sheet found on page 82 in Chapter 6, so they know exactly how their mandalas will be evaluated. It is important for students to know ahead of time what is desired so they can work toward meeting, or going beyond, criteria set out.
- Brainstorm possible category titles for the second circle on the blackboard (e.g., Family, Hobbies, Likes, Dislikes, Future Plans, Favorite Subjects,

Mandala

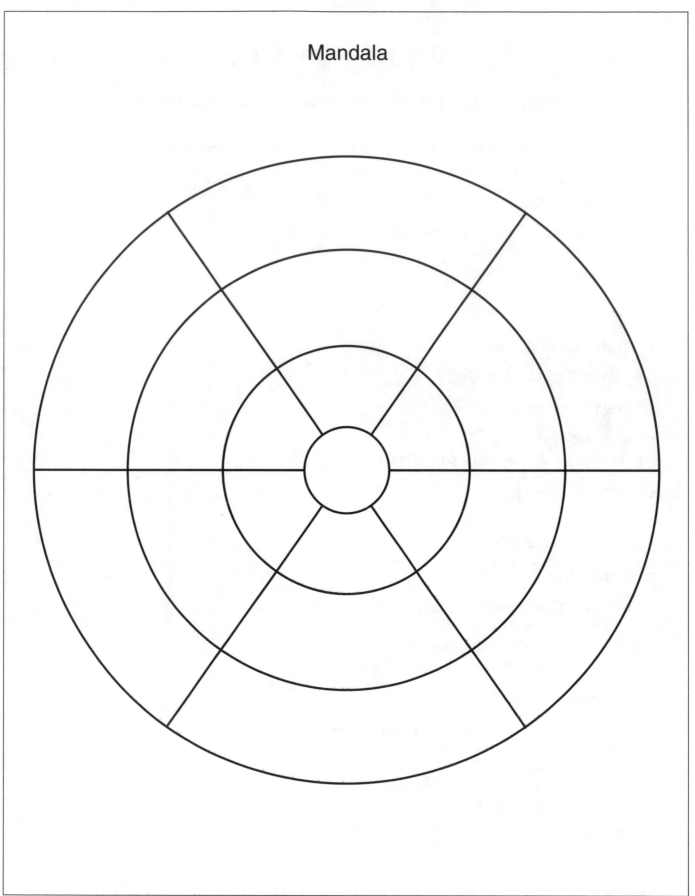

Criteria for Mandalas

1. PRINT AS IF ON A LINE, SO THAT THE MANDALA CAN BE READ FROM ONE POSITION

- Do not follow the shape of the section or turn paper around when printing
- Print or write against a ruler, but do not draw lines

2. NEATNESS IS IMPORTANT

- Be neat in printing, drawing or coloring
- Use pencil to print or write
- Use pencil crayon to color
- Do not color over words
- Outline sections if you wish

3. CORRECT SPELLING

- Check and correct all spelling

4. CENTRE CIRCLE

- Identify the title or topic
- Print clearly and start with a capital letter

5. SECOND CIRCLE

- Write category names
- Start with a capital letter

6. THIRD CIRCLE

- Give information on each category via notes or details
- Use dashes for note form
- Be brief, but thorough in note taking
- Use phrases rather than single words if possible

7. OUTSIDE CIRCLE

- Include illustrations showing content of each section
- Color, including the background
- Label, only if necessary

8. BOTTOM RIGHT CORNER

- Write your name

Best Moments, Friends, Favorite Foods, Talents, etc.). I normally instruct students to use Family as one of their categories, and give them a choice for the other five.

- Hand out the blank mandalas and ask the students to create their own "Me" mandala. Instruct the students to begin with the center circle by printing their name in the center or, if using a photo, tell them to wait until the mandala is totally completed and then to cut their face out of the photo and glue it into the center.

- Circulate around the classroom as students begin working on their mandalas, helping them to remember criteria such as using a ruler for writing, dashes for notes, etc. Stress neatness, as overall appearance is important on a mandala.
- Give students several periods over the next few days to complete their mandalas. Go over expected criteria again, if necessary.
- Pre-cut a variety of colored pieces of construction paper (11" x 17") into squares. When students complete their mandala, have them cut their mandala out and glue it onto a square of paper.
- Pass out self-evaluation sheets and have students evaluate their mandalas. I suggest you do this together, one criteria at a time, so you can explain each one, and help students determine the rating they might give. Initially, students who have not had practice in self-evaluating, will rate their work unrealistically. With experience using criteria-based evaluation, students improve in their ability to look at their own work in much the same way you, the teacher, would. Using criteria helps students to learn what makes up a mark, and discover specifically what areas need improvement.
- Ask students to hand in both their mounted mandala, as well as their self-evaluation sheet.
- Place the mounted mandalas up on the bulletin board for all to see. What a great way to get to know each other!
- Transfer this learning to create mandalas on other topics as the year progresses, such as the elements of a novel.

Learning Journal Cover Collage

Learning journals, which are described in more detail in the next section, promote student reflection on their learning and give them a place to explore ideas, opinions, etc. Before they actually get into writing in their journals, I usually have them prepare a cover collage early in the year. The purpose of doing this collage is threefold:

- To help students clarify their own interests, strengths and values
- To learn about collage as an art form
- To create an interesting cover for an important book

I usually have the students use a student Keytab-type notebook for this activity, as the cover is removed, decorated, then stapled back on. The collage becomes the cover for this notebook, which is titled "Learning Journal" (or Learning Log, Reflection Book, Thinking Log, The Very Important Book, etc.).

Materials

- Keytab-type notebook cover (remove with staple remover)
- Old magazines

- Scissors
- Glue
- Photo of student (may be glued onto cover, as part of the collage, or on the inside first page of the book with the written explanation of the cover)

Directions

- Ask the students to write their name in pencil on the top-right inside page of one of their notebooks, then give it to you. Use a staple remover to remove the front covers of the books, and store the inside pages until students need them.
- Plan for a long period of time (at least an hour) to get started on the collage. On the day of the lesson, tell students that they will be creating the cover for a very special book that will be used throughout the year in a variety of ways. Explain that it will not only chronicle their school year, it will also give them insights as to what kind of a person they were at this age, what they thought about things, what they learned, who their friends were and what was important to them. Tell them that the cover of this book will be laminated so that it can be kept in good condition.
- Ask students to think about what kinds of pictures represent who they are. Brainstorm ideas on board.
- Decide, as the teacher, what the students should focus on. You may decide to have students simply focus on things they like, which makes it easy to find representative photos. However, I like the covers to go a little deeper, showing what students believe, what issues they feel strongly about, and what dreams or plans they might have for the future. Guide such a discussion by asking students:
  - What things might represent how you think?
  - What things might represent what you believe?
  - What things might represent your hopes and dreams?
  It is definitely more difficult for students to find photographs that represent thoughts, feelings and beliefs, but I like to present this challenge to them to extend their thinking and to give more depth to their personal response.
- Have students record their personal information. Then, ask them to think of what pictures they might find that will show these ideas. This will serve as a guide and help to keep the students focused on what types of pictures they are looking for.
- Discuss collage as an art form. Show any examples you may have on hand. Ask the students if they are able to tell the theme or message of the collage? What do they think it is about? Ask the students what they notice about how the collage was created.
- Go over the whole procedure the students will use to create their collage to give them the "big picture" before they begin. Show students how they can rip pictures out of the magazines, and stockpile them. Then, when they think they have enough, demonstrate how they can cut the pictures and find a pleasing arrangement on top of their cover. Explain to them that once they have enough to completely cover the area, they may begin playing around with them until they decide on a good arrangement. At that point, they can glue the pictures onto the cover, making sure that they remember which is the front and which is the back.
- Explain that if a student is using a photo as part of the collage, no name is needed on the cover. However, if a student chooses to glue the photo on the

inside page of the book with the written comment, tell students to also look for the letters of their name, in any size, shape or color, when they are leafing through the magazines. They will then glue their name onto the front of the book, on top of the collage.

- Go over the criteria you will use for evaluating the collages if evaluating them, and show students a copy of the evaluation that will be used. Explain to the students that they will also be writing about their cover and that part of the evaluation will be on how well the cover illustrates what is written in the explanation (see Chapter 6 for assessment ideas).
- Remind students that personal collages form an image about the essence of a person. To prevent students from simply cutting out pictures they like the look of, encourage depth, and focus them on the elements they chose as important.
- Give students adequate time to collect pictures, to practise arranging them, and to complete the collage.
- Get covers laminated, then re-staple them to the notebooks with a long-arm stapler.
- Evaluate the collages, if desired.
- Have the students write about their cover page on the first page in their notebook, explaining how it tells about them. Encourage students to save this one! They will greatly enjoy reading it in the years to come.

My cover tells a lot about me. As you can see, I LOVE animals! The cougar, bear, elk and wolf show that I love wild animals. The dogs, cats, horses, cows and rabbit show that I also love tame animals, and that I enjoy having pets. My favorite animals are dogs. When I grow up, I want to be a vet or work with animals. The canoe and sunset pictures show that I really like the outdoors, and I like to go camping and canoeing with my family. The bike shows that I also like to go biking. The fruit shows that I live in the Okanagan, where lots of fruit grows. The word Saskatchewan tells that we own a farm there and we go back there every summer. That's where my Dad's family is. The whole cover shows that nature is important to me and I think we need to take good care of our environment.

Learning Journals

Learning involves reflection. It is important for you to take the time to guide the students in thinking about themselves as learners, to set goals for themselves, and to express opinions and thoughts in writing. Whether called a "learning journal" or titled otherwise, this is the book into which students are asked to make entries on a regular basis all year long. It is the one book which best shows their growth throughout the school year, both as a person and as a student.

Materials

- Notebook (see activity for a collage cover described in the last section)

Directions

- Hand out notebooks early in the year that will serve as students' learning journals. This might be a notebook with a laminated collage cover, as described in the last section.
- Explain that they will use this book to:
  - set term goals and evaluate them
  - document and write opinions about school events or class activities
  - write to learning partners
  - write to parents
  - reflect upon their work and their learning
  - evaluate progress they have made
  - store photographs taken during the year (with captions)
- Provide the students with stems to start their writing initially. However, as students become accustomed to recording and knowing the expectations for length and depth, they are soon able to write excellent responses with little guidance.
- Send this book home weekly or monthly, with a student letter to parents telling about their activities at school. The parents are then asked to write a note in the book in response to what their child has written. I like to send the book halfway through each term, so parents can see the goals their child has set, and can read other entries. I have students self-evaluate their progress, or note improvements, and comment on aspects of the classroom. The learning journal going back and forth in this way increases communication between school and home, and helps parents understand more about their child's classroom environment.

Student-of-the-Week

After seeing the success a former colleague, Julie Witt, experienced in using a "Student-of-the-Week" program in her primary classroom, I modified the program to meet the demands of the curriculum for the students in my grade 5 and 6 classes. There is very little preparation needed on the teacher's part to get this type of program underway. I normally begin during the last week in September or the first week in October, after other start-up activities for class meetings are completed.

Since instituting this program, I have discovered many important benefits that go well beyond the building of students' self-esteem. This program has many advantages for the whole class. Student-of-the-Week provides an opportunity to:

- Develop and evaluate students' public-speaking ability
- Assess students' willingness to participate in discussions
- Encourage good listening and question-asking skills
- Help build students' personal profiles of strengths, talents and interests
- Guide students in investigating possible career choices
- Increase students' knowledge of their community
- Create a liaison between the community and the school
- Increase positive public relations amongst the stakeholders in education (i.e., parents, schools and communities)
- Teach and have the students practise appropriate audience behavior

Materials

- Prepared bulletin board for student use, preferably with a counter below
- Copies of a letter to go home with students (see sample on following page)
- Guides for introducing and thanking guests (see samples in margin)
- Art materials for making thank-you cards, envelopes, etc.
- Copies of career/occupation grids and hobby/interest grids (optional—see samples on page 73)
- Copies of a class list for assessing student participation in discussions (optional—see Chapter 6)
- Camera to take photos of the students with their guests (optional)

Directions

- Prepare a few items and teach a few skills before beginning the program. These include:
  - setting up a bulletin board with a title and a border
  - writing a letter to go home and photocopying enough to keep on file for the whole class
  - scheduling the time for guests to come in into your weekly timetable (e.g., first thing Monday morning; after lunch on Friday)
  - distributing and discussing the guides for introducing and thanking guests with the students
  - teaching students how to write a thank-you note
  - preparing grid papers for guest information (optional)
  - preparing a class list for assessing student participation in discussions (optional)
  - going over the etiquette for being a good audience
- Introduce the concept of Student-of-the-Week to the class. Outline for students what their responsibilities will be throughout their week. For example:

  Monday
  - set up a bulletin board and counter display (including a sign with their name) with items that reflect their interests, talents, etc.
  - speak to the class about their family and explain how the items they have brought in tell about them
  - answer questions that the class poses

  Thursday (or whatever day you decide)
  - be the leader for class meeting (optional)

  Friday
  - bring a guest into the class to talk about a job or hobby
  - introduce and thank the guest
  - write a thank-you note to the previous week's guest

  Make sure that students understand that it is their responsibility to invite a guest with an interesting job or hobby to come in at the designated time on their week.
- Encourage the students to listen respectfully during guests' presentations and to ask pertinent questions afterward.
- Take a photograph of each student with his or her guest (optional). You may wish to get doubles made, and put one in the student's learning journal, and the other on the bulletin board. Eventually, this second photo can go into the class photo album.

Student-of-the-Week Program

Dear Parents,

Your child, _____, has been selected to be Student-of-the-Week for the week of _____.

On Monday, the student will set up a bulletin board/counter display of any samples of work, projects, treasures, memorabilia, etc., that he or she would like the class to see during the week, and will speak to the class about himself or herself.

On _____, the student will have the opportunity to be the leader for a class meeting, during which time he or she will receive an encouragement from each classmate.

On _____, from _____ to _____, the student will bring a guest to class. The student may wish to bring a parent or relative who has a job that can be demonstrated or explained (e.g., a carpenter showing simple tools and how they work or how to build a toy boat, or a baker showing how to ice a cake). The guest might be someone who speaks another language and can teach the class how to count to ten or say a few words. It may be someone who is able to tell stories or demonstrate an art or craft idea, or show slides of travels. Any ethnic or cultural foods, clothing, customs or games would be most interesting. As part of the half-hour guest presentation, your child may also wish to demonstrate a skill, a musical talent or a collection.

This experience will give students the opportunity to learn about different careers and hobbies, and to see people as unique individuals, each with special talents, interests, culture and family. It improves students' listening skills, questioning skills, writing skills and public-speaking skills. It creates a community feeling in the class and helps each student to feel important and part of the group.

If you have any concerns or questions, or any problems with the scheduled time, please call me. Thank you for your participation in this program.

Sincerely,

_____

- Guide students in filling in a grid similar to one of the ones shown below after each guest has gone, as well as in making an entry into their learning journal describing what they learned and whether or not this job or hobby would appeal to them and why.

Careers and Occupations

Occupation	Education or Training	Skills Required	Type of Job	Interest Me? Why?

Hobbies and Interests

Interest or Hobby	Supplies Needed	Skills Required	Things You Can Make or Do	Interest Me? Why?

- Use the information on completed careers and occupations grids to guide students later in the year in categorizing types of jobs based upon whether they are jobs that mainly require one to work with:
  - people
  - machines and tools
  - information

  Encourage students to consider their personal preferences, as well as the education requirements and skills needed to narrow down some career possibilities that might suit them. You may wish to have students research a particular area of interest for a presentation that could be part of a "career fair."
- Invite the guests to a volunteer tea at the end of the year where students participate in performances for the adults to thank them for their contributions.

Building Community

The following activities promote student interaction, unite the class and help create a "we" feeling in the classroom. Some are done over short periods of time, while others are ongoing throughout the year.

People Search

I think class meetings help people express their feelings for other people.

Student, age 11

This idea, adapted from *Catch Them Thinking* by James Bellanca and Robin Fogarty (1986), has many possible applications. I like to use it as a "mixer" activity on the first or second day of school. Not knowing all the students coming into my classroom, I simply try to make the content generic enough so that it can apply to students of the age entering my classroom that year. This activity:

- Encourages students to use first names when addressing each other
- Promotes interaction of students
- Allows students to learn something about each other
- Lets students have fun

Materials

- Class set of copies of a People Search (see sample on the opposite page)
- Clipboards, if available

Directions

- Distribute copies of the search sheet. Read over each box together with the students.
- Explain to the students how the activity will proceed. Tell them that they will need to:
    - get up out of their seats and circulate around the room, asking people questions from the sheet
    - try to fill in as many squares as they can in the time allowed
    - find a different person for each square
    - address each student by name (e.g., "John, do you ... ?")
    - ask people fitting the criteria for squares to write their names in the appropriate boxes (I find this saves a lot of time as students do not know how to spell each other's names this early in the school year)
    - try to complete the sheet in ten minutes
- Set the timer, and tell students to begin. They may ask you questions also.
- Stop the students after ten minutes to see how they are doing and extend the time, if necessary. Let the students know when they must stop.
- Invite the students to share the information learned on the sheet. You may wish the students to use this information for other purposes such as for generating graphs in mathematics.

The Way We Like Our Class to Be

Many teacher resources discuss the importance of establishing a code of conduct or set of guidelines that the class agrees upon as the classroom "rules" for the coming year. I like to incorporate this with the development of charts outlining the characteristics of a "good" student and a "good" teacher, with what we believe to be a "good" classroom. A delightful picture book I like to use to develop some of these ideas is *Lilly's Purple Plastic Purse,* a story about a little girl who loves school and her teacher, until her inappropriate behavior causes some problems.

Materials

- *Lilly's Purple Plastic Purse,* or other story exploring behavior at school
- Chart paper

Directions

- Read students the story you have selected. If using *Lilly's Purple Plastic Purse,* you might want to bring in the items Lilly brings to school in the book (i.e., purse, quarters, sunglasses) to prompt predictions about the story content before reading it. Ask students if they think Lilly—or the main character in your chosen book—is a good student. Encourage

People Search

Find someone who ...

likes corn on the cob	has been to a circus	has a birthday in the same month as yours	has more than 5 CDs
went camping this summer	has read a Harry Potter book	has rollerblades	has a public library card
lives on a farm	has a trampoline	plays on a baseball team	has the same eye color as you
has been to DisneyWorld	has 4 kids in his or her family	has an allergy	knows the answer to $(4 \times 3) - 12 =$

students to identify what characteristics Lilly—or another character—possess that make her—or him—a good student.

- Lead students into developing the criteria for what they consider to be a good student by brainstorming attributes on chart paper.
- Combine or generalize concepts that are repetitive in nature.
- Give each student three sticky dots, and instruct them to place the dots beside the characteristics they think represent the qualities that make a good student.
- Print about five characteristics that have the most support on a chart.
- Use this chart to assist in student self-evaluations at various times during the year.
- Repeat this process for the qualities of a good teacher, beginning with the qualities Mr. Slinger—or another "teacher" book character—possess. Use the list to evaluate yourself.

Criteria for a Good Student	Criteria for a Good Teacher
Listens and pays attention	Is organized
Has a positive attitude	Makes learning fun
Is respectful and polite	Listens to ideas and is open-minded
Is responsible and organized	Has a positive attitude
Works/plays cooperatively	Is firm, but fair

We Like a Classroom Where ...

1. We show respect for others
2. We listen when someone is speaking
3. We take responsibility for our actions
4. We work together cooperatively
5. We strive to do our personal best

- Ask students what they think the characteristics of a great classroom are. Again, follow a similar series of steps to the ones outlined above to come up with what the students want their classroom to be. Post these beliefs on a chart like the one shown that the class can refer to and "live by" during the year.
- Revisit these criteria at various points throughout the year, and revise if necessary.

Stocking Exchange

The following activity of preparing and exchanging stockings culminates on the final day of school before dismissal for the winter holidays. At this point, each student receives a stocking made for them by a classmate, stuffed with goodies from all of their classmates. This activity helps to solidify the community feeling that is probably already well established at this point in the year.

When the stockings are hung along the blackboard, the care and attention each student has put into their making is evident, and pride glows on the students' faces. I am always amazed at the creativity displayed in the decorating, and the joy expressed in the receiving, no matter how elaborate or primitive the product. My students and I just love this activity, enjoying the camaraderie of a "family" gathering and the giving and receiving of the small tokens placed by students in each other's stockings.

Materials

- Cardboard stocking templates
- Fabric
- Decorating materials
- A homemade or bought stocking stuffer—enough for the whole class

Directions

- Put the idea for a stocking exchange into the class meeting box about a month before the winter holidays. When called upon at the meeting, explain to the students that:
    - each person will draw the name of another student in the class, which will be kept secret
    - each student will make a large holiday stocking for the other person at home
    - stockings will be cut out of fabric, sewn on a sewing machine (with a loop for hanging) and decorated
    - everyone will bring their stockings to school by the Monday of the last week of school, and you will hide them away until the last day
    - patterns to make stockings will be supplied, as well as letter tracers and felt to cut out names
    - students who can, will bring extra fabric, decorative touches, etc. to share
    - parents will need to help with sewing
    - all stockings will be different—some elaborate and some less so—depending upon how much help students get from parents and availability of materials, etc.
    - students will be required to stuff all of the stockings on the final day of school with an item that they will bring for the whole class—either bought or homemade (e.g., chocolate kisses, pencils, erasers, crafts, etc.)
- Answer any questions brought up at the class meeting to clarify the suggestion, then ask for a show of hands of those interested.
- Cut up a class list and have the students draw names, if they vote to do the activity. Set due dates for the stockings and stuffers.
- Clip cardboard stocking patterns to the board with a numbered list below where students can sign them out. Have them erase their name when they return a pattern.

- Send a notice home to parents, such as the one shown here, informing them of the activity, and the need for their assistance.

Sample Letter to Parents for Stocking Exchange

Dear Parents/Guardians:

The students have decided they would like to take part in a holiday activity where everyone makes a stocking for someone else in the class at home. Each child has drawn the name of someone in the class who he or she is to make the stocking for (it's a secret!). Stockings must be sewn by machine. If you do not have access to a sewing machine, your child's stocking may be sewn by parents who volunteer to help out.

Students have begun to sign out the stocking pattern to take home at night, where they will need to cut it out of fabric. Any type of material will work as long as it is big enough for the pattern. Some students will be bringing in fabric to share. I also have some extra fabric at school, as well as felt for the letters for students' names.

On the last day before the holiday, each student will also be required to bring in a class set of an item to fill all of the stockings. This will give each child an individual handmade stocking filled with an assortment of goodies. Stockings can be filled with homemade or bought items, ____ of the same thing. This is not meant to be an expensive activity, and I have encouraged the class to think of things they can do or make for each other if they do not wish to buy something. In past years, we have had a huge variety of items, including poems, pencils, homemade fudge, crafts, chocolate kisses, etc.

Thank you in advance for your assistance with this activity.

Sincerely,

_____

Stockings due: _____
Stuffers due: _____

- Suggest to the students that they can decorate the stocking they make with items cut out of felt that represent the interests of the person for whom they are making the stocking, or use bits and pieces of lace, sequins, buttons, or other simple materials they may have at home to decorate it.
- Leave lettering templates and felt out the week before stockings are due so students can cut out names to glue onto the stockings.
- Remind students to sew a sturdy hanger on their stocking.
- Put stockings in a safe place, hidden away, as the students bring them in. Keep a master list showing who each student is making a stocking for. You can use this to check names off as the stockings are brought in, so you know which students have not completed stockings.
- Make sure to write the students' names on their bags, and check their names off on a list, as stuffers are brought in too.
- String a wire from one end of a double blackboard to the other, with a center support to hang the stockings on.

- Hang the stockings "by the blackboard with care" on the day the exchange is to take place. This will be the first time students see the stocking that has been made for them. There is great excitement in the class during the day as students admire the beautiful array of stockings.
- Encourage the students on the day of the exchange to appreciate the efforts of their classmates, and to focus on the giving, not the appearance of the gift.
- Hand out the bags of stuffers students have given you, and instruct one small group of students at a time to go up and stuff each stocking with the items they brought. While groups are "stuffing," the rest of the class can be doing other holiday activities that you, or the students, have prepared.
- Take down the stuffed stockings, one by one, and pass them out. Students should wait to open them until everyone's stocking has been delivered.
- Say, "You can now open your stockings!" and watch the excitement and glee as everyone dumps out the contents of their stocking and examines the treasures within!
- Allow a few minutes for students to fully enjoy seeing what they have received. I usually tell them they can eat three things only, and the rest is to go home. I like the parents to see what the stockings contain.
- Give the students the opportunity to guess who made their stocking for them. One of my classes came up with the idea of putting a folded piece of paper into the bottom of each stocking, with a poem or rhyme giving a clue as to who made the stocking. This greatly enhanced the "guessing" of who made the stocking.
- Lead the students in guessing who made their stocking by calling upon one student to begin. The class will have decided in a class meeting how many guesses to give. The usual is two, but if clues are given, students may decide to allow only one guess. If the student guesses incorrectly, the person who made the stocking stands to identify himself or herself. As the makers of the stockings are identified, they give their learning journal to the person they made the stocking for.
- Tell the students that after the exchange, they will write a thank-you note to the person who made their stocking. Instruct students to be specific about naming something they really liked about their stocking when thanking its maker.
- Return the learning journals to their rightful owners, and allow the students time to read their notes.
- Have the students take their stocking and contents home.

Dear Marie:

Thank you for making my stocking. I like the way you put the soccer ball on it because soccer is my favorite sport. You did a great job decorating it too. I really like it.

John

6

Celebrating Success

As the year progresses, the many benefits of class meetings become evident, as student growth is seen in many areas. Celebrating the accomplishments, achievements and successes of both individuals and the class as a group is an important part of recognizing gains that have been made.

Assessment

A wealth of data for student assessment can be provided with the use of:

- Checklists
- Criteria-based evaluation (peer, self, teacher)
- Goal-setting and evaluation
- Journal writing
- Teacher observation

Checklists

Student participation in class meetings and activities such as Student-of-the-Week presentations may form part of your assessment of a student's skills in listening and speaking—two of the four components of language arts. Using a class list, place a check mark each time a student contributes to a discussion by making a comment or asking a pertinent question. Over the course of a term, such a checklist is very helpful in determining student growth. Comparisons over consecutive terms generate clear data, useful in evaluating student progress.

Student	Monday Presentation	Class Meetings	Guests
Allen	✓	✓	✓✓
Bill	✓✓✓✓✓	✓✓✓✓✓	✓✓✓✓

Criteria-based Evaluation

Students will aim to reach whatever expectations are set before them. Knowing what is expected before beginning an activity offers students the opportunity to work toward meeting these, or, in the case of some students, surpassing them.

Whenever possible, involve students in choosing which criteria their work will be evaluated by. Sometimes, you may have particular criteria which are non-negotiable. Share these with the students. At the same time, ask them what criteria they think would be important to include. Engaging the students in developing criteria not only focuses the activity to follow, it helps them to understand the important characteristics of what they are about to do.

A typical example of a self evaluation based on criteria is the sheet shown on the following page, which can be used to evaluate students' "Me" Mandalas. Criteria sheets such as this help students develop a realistic sense of how marks are arrived at, encouraging them to pinpoint specific areas of strength and weakness in their work. The use of criteria greatly enhances a student's ability to be successful, as it provides a clear sense of purpose and direction, and indicates to the student which parts of the whole may need improving.

Another example, using a slightly different format, might be used to evaluate oral presentations. As students gain experience and a comfort level in class meetings, they begin to feel more confident expressing their thoughts and feelings in front of a group. Beginning with the Personality Pack presentations early in the year (see Chapter 5), facility in speaking in front of a large group can be rated and growth can be noted over the course of the year using a sheet such as the one shown on page 83.

My school focuses on students striving for their personal best. Posters in each classroom list the criteria for determining "personal best," providing a visual aid to students. Each term, I have students self evaluate in this area, using the form shown on page 84. Students who have chosen "doing my personal best" as a term goal—this is discussed in the next section—will find this checklist of criteria helpful as it focuses their efforts.

Goal-setting and Evaluation

Each term, I guide students in setting goals for themselves, outlining a plan they will use to reach them, and finding a method of "proving" that goals have been reached. Students do this work in their learning journals. Growth seen in the many learning outcomes affected by continued participation in class meetings is another way to assess their effectiveness.

Goals are set in three main areas at the start of a term, then evaluated near the end. These include:

- *Academic goals*—mastering specific concepts or skills in particular subject areas
- *Work habit goals*—demonstrating organization, displaying good penmanship, completing homework, focusing, following directions, producing neat work, staying on task, completing work on time, following classroom routines, keeping desk and materials in order, following criteria for assignments, etc.
- *Personal goals*—getting along with others, making friends, working in a group, managing anger, putting hand up to speak instead of calling out, participating in class meetings, speaking in front of the group, cooperating with others, having a positive attitude, getting to know learning partners, etc.

Evaluating a Mandala

Name: _____   Date: _____

Topic or Assignment: MANDALA _____

Givens:
- complete (all sections filled in)
- colored
- name written on it

Criteria	5 Excellent	4 Very Good	3 Good	2 Satisfactory	1 Minimally Acceptable	Student	Teacher	Weight
• All writing done in one direction, as on a line								
• Quantity and quality of information, main ideas								× 2
• Note-making ability								
• Neatness in writing and drawing								× 2
• Overall appearance and effort								

Overall, my _mandala_ is

     5   **4**   **3**   **2**   **1**
    Ex **VG** **G**   **S**   **MA**

I am most proud of the way I _____

_____

Next time, to improve, I could _____

_____

Teacher evaluation and comments **Ex VG G S MA** _____

_____

Criteria for Oral Presentation

Name: _____ Date: _____

Criteria	Rating
Voice	
• volume (loud)	1　2　3　4　5
• clear (good enunciaton)	1　2　3　4　5
• good pacing (not too fast, pauses)	1　2　3　4　5
• good expression	1　2　3　4　5
Eye contact (pans audience, only glances at notes)	1　2　3　4　5
Poise (comfortable stance, at ease, stands tall, looks confident)	1　2　3　4　5
Organization	
• shows evidence of planning	1　2　3　4　5
• knows the material well	1　2　3　4　5
Content (tells enough information about topic)	1　2　3　4　5

Total _____
45

Comments:

Areas for improvement:

Personal Best Self Evaluation

Name: _____   Date: _____

Criteria	Almost Always	Some of the Time	Not Yet
• I have a positive attitude			
• I listen and pay attention			
• I follow directions and criteria			
• I produce good quality work			
• I do my homework			
• I follow classroom routines and expectations			
• I follow school routines and expectations			
• I treat other students with respect			
• I treat teachers and other adults with respect			
• I show respect for property (my own and others')			
• I put my best effort into all I do			

One thing I feel I have done really well this term is _____

_____

Of all the criteria listed above, the one area I need to focus on for improvement next term is

_____

_____

Before students sit down to set their goals in the above three areas, they will need some guidance. You may wish to:

- Engage the students in a discussion about what is planned for the term by listing topics and ideas on the blackboard to guide students in choosing goals
- Tell students to divide a page in their learning journal into three equal sections, with the appropriate goal headings underlined
- Provide the three sentence stems needed to write about each goal:
  - My (academic) goal this term is ...
  - My plan is to ...
  - I will know I have reached my goal when ...

Sample Term 2 Goals

Academic Goal

My academic goal this term is to understand fractions and decimals better.
My plan is to:

1. listen when lessons are given
2. ask questions if I don't understand something
3. work hard when completing assignments

I will know I have reached my goal when I can look at a question and know how to do it and I can see an improvement on my marks on quizzes and tests.

Work Habit Goal

My work habit goal this term is to pay attention in class.
My plan is to:

1. look at the person who is speaking
2. not be fiddling with things
3. sit still and listen

I will know I have achieved my goal when I feel like I know more about what's going on in the class, and I know what to do, and the teacher doesn't always have to remind me to pay attention.

Personal Goal

My personal goal this term is to be able to speak in front of the class.
My plan is to:

1. put my hand up more in class meetings
2. ask questions when we have a guest
3. do an oral presentation for my social studies report instead of a written one

I will know I have achieved my goal when I feel more comfortable speaking in front of the whole class and I can check with the teacher to see if I have more check marks over the term for speaking.

Near the end of the term, the students will need to revisit their goals. Instruct them to:

- Divide a page once again into three sections, in order to prepare for the evaluation of goals

- Write the title, "Term ___ Goal Evaluation" at the top of the page, and the three headings below
- Use stems such as the following to record their progress in reaching goals:
  - My (academic) goal this term was to ...
  - I have/have partly/have not reached it. I know this because ...
  - I think my plan was ...
  - I think/feel ...

Sample Goal Evaluation

Personal Goal

My personal goal this term was to speak in front of the class. I have reached this goal. I know this because I feel way more comfortable saying things in class and whenever we have a presentation, I have been asking lots of questions. I asked the teacher to show me the checklist for participation, and I had way more check marks this term. I feel good about reaching this goal, because I have always been shy, but now I just take a deep breath and put my hand up.

Journal Writing

Class meetings have been my favorite part of the class! Class meeting responses are quite a hard subject for me to write down my thoughts. I have enjoyed writing responses because they help me learn about expressing my feelings more.

Student, age 10

My students often stop, think, talk, write and share. Student reflection is a valid evidence of progress. Personal responses to events and activities, academic and otherwise, not only form part of my assessment of student progress, but help students articulate their growth and improvements, leading to self understanding.

Talking and writing about their experiences in class meetings leads students to introspection and discoveries, strengthening their understanding of the impact the process is having both on themselves personally and on the class as a whole. When students are unaccustomed to journal writing, providing stems with which to begin their entries guides their thinking and provides a platform upon which to build personal response. Here are some that I have found effective for eliciting insightful responses:

- Today in the class meeting, I noticed ...
- I think class meetings are great because ...
- One thing I learned in the class meeting today is ...
- I notice that at class meetings, I am getting better at ...
- When solving a problem, the hardest thing is ...
- To be a good problem solver, a person has to ...
- The steps I would take if I had a problem are ...
- When I was the leader of the class meeting today, I felt ...
- Class meetings affect the whole class by ...

Sample Reflections from Journals

When you're the person that talks in front of the class, it helps you learn how to speak in front of a large group of people.

I think that laughing at people when they say something lowers the other person's self-esteem. When I get laughed at, inside I am really angry.

I notice that lots of kids like to tease other people, or hide things or bug them. When that happens, kids try to solve their problem first, but if that problem does not get solved, you need some help and that is where class meetings begin.

Students, ages 10 to 12

Expectations for depth of response and content are easily established with criteria, decided upon and shared at the outset, and used for evaluation purposes upon completion. Teacher resources contain a large number and types of forms that one can use to guide students' metacognitive thinking. As students become more adept at written reflection, and know what is expected, they will need very little guidance or direction when expressing themselves in written form.

Teacher Observation

Student behaviors observed during class meetings provide another important insight into skill development in relation to curriculum goals. Observation provides the opportunity to note progress in areas that are often difficult to assess. For example, is a student:

- Gaining self-confidence?
- Demonstrating good listening skills?
- Staying on task and remaining focused for long periods of time?
- Following expectations for behavior?
- Disagreeing with others in a respectful manner?
- Taking responsibility for behavior by owning up to it?
- Realizing that his/her behavior affects others?
- Contributing to discussions?
- Asking appropriate questions?
- Expressing an opinion and stating reasons to support it?
- Generating creative solutions?
- Suggesting logical, reasonable consequences?
- Piggybacking ideas from others?
- Synthesizing, paraphrasing and summarizing?
- Making choices based on criteria?
- Taking a stand even when he or she is in the minority?
- Feeling like part of the group?
- Respecting others' right to speak and to have opinions?
- Showing sensitivity to others?
- Giving compliments to others?
- Showing cooperation?
- Volunteering for committees?

With class meetings held on a regular basis over the space of a school year, growth in students' social/emotional development, their level of social responsibility, and their intellectual development can easily be seen, providing valuable assessment information.

Celebrations

During the course of a school year, in addition to recognizing personal achievements, the students as a group need to acknowledge their own and each other's accomplishments in the form of celebrations. The celebration of a class goal being reached might take the form of a special event, time earned to do self-chosen activities, or other student-planned ideas. Celebrations take place also to honor and affirm the success individual students and the class are experiencing as they perform day-to-day tasks or take part in ongoing programs.

Many of the following celebrations are initially suggested and discussed in class meetings.

Celebrating Class Goal Attainment

In my classroom, when classroom routines need to be learned or on-task behavior is a focus, we pick a method of recording each time the class is successful in meeting the goal for the time period or the day. The class has a certain, agreed-upon, amount of time in which to reach the goal. The reward is a celebration.

Celebrations are sometimes chosen by me, sometimes by the students, and more often, by all of us together. It is important to:

- Itemize and record the expected behaviors clearly in written form
- Specify a short time period, no more than one month, to reach a goal
- Be consistent and fair in recording progress

Some great ideas for recording progress in attaining class goals are ones that have been shared with me by colleagues, or ones the students and I have "invented" in class meetings. In each case, every time the students as a class exhibit expected behaviors they are working on, a "point" is given, which can take different forms. A few of my favorites are:

- A large thermometer, laminated, with lines that are filled in each time the class exhibits expected behaviors.
- A grid chart of boxes which are crossed off or checked.
- A jar into which one spoon of candy (e.g., jelly beans) is placed each time goal behavior is shown. This one is best done weekly, with candy shared at week's end. (It provides for a good math lesson when calculating how many candies each student will receive, but it can be quite expensive!).
- A jar into which a scoop of a non-edible material, such as marbles, is placed each time goal behavior is demonstrated. When the jar is full, the class enjoys a celebration decided upon together.

The fun part in recognizing the attainment of a class goal is to decide upon a celebration. In class meeting discussions, students come up with many ideas, such as:

- Sharing earned goodies
- Having popcorn and watching a video (if deemed appropriate)
- Choosing an activity they wish to do such as a game they want to play together, or an event a student committee plans

Celebrating Being Part of a Group

Class meetings are definitely the forum where great ideas are spawned, leading the class down many exciting roads during the school year. Sharing fun activities helps the class to bond and celebrate the "family unit," as well as provides a base upon which relationships are deepened.

I find that I need do little in this area, as the students come up with so many suggestions on their own, especially after looking through class photo albums from previous years. A few ideas that I notice are repeated each year are:

- Wacky Hair Day (and other "weird and wonderful" days)

Sample Class Goal List

Class Goal: to be on task

Time Frame: 3 weeks

Celebration: "center time" choices for 20 minutes first thing in the morning for a week

Expected Behaviors:
- Sit in desk after bells
- Begin work, or choose quiet activity
- Be quiet during transition times
- Do not disturb others when working on own
- Be on task when working together
- Line up quietly when going elsewhere

- Tobogganing (or sliding on inner tubes) at a nearby hill
- Seasonal activities such as valentine exchanges, Hallowe'en creative costume competitions, etc.
- Activities with our little buddies
- Potluck luncheons

The two final ideas are described in more detail below.

Buddies

My older students love having a little grade one buddy. Throughout the year, we meet weekly, for one period, and do a wide range of activities together, including reading, adding and subtracting, doing projects, measuring, weighing, drawing, coloring, cutting, running, planting, keyboarding and dancing. The older students are responsible for helping, and also for modeling, for their little partner. Many of the activities are suggested and planned in weekly class meetings.

We always end our year together with a celebration—usually involving games and food! In recent years we have gone to a local park to swim, play parachute games, and have a barbecue. The year-end barbecue is a celebration of the positive relationship students have developed with each other. In a class meeting, a committee is formed to organize the event. The student committee:

- Plans what activities will take place and makes up a schedule
- Writes a notice to go home to parents asking for their help
- Posts a sign-up list for food
- Organizes which games will be played
- Collects equipment for games
- Keeps both classes informed of plans
- Arranges for food and equipment to be taken to the park
- Organizes for setting up and cleaning up at the park

Last year, the students swam, then ate, then played cooperative games with the parachute, as well as small group games of choice. A good time was had by all! Buddies bring out the best in kids, and help students feel they are part of a special group of friends.

Potluck Luncheons

Food is often the center of gatherings with friends, and the classroom is no exception. My students love having potlucks that are theme-based, usually focusing on a unit of study. Plans for a potluck are made in a class meeting, a date is set, and a committee is struck to work out the details. Students put up a sign-up sheet outlining specific types of courses, and the number of students that should sign up. Notices are sent home to inform parents and ask for their help.

If students do not suggest a potluck, put the suggestion into the class meeting box yourself! Potlucks are not only fun, they:

- Get students involved in planning and organizing an event
- Help students learn the benefits of working together and reaching a goal
- Provide the opportunity for students to play "host" to guests
- Give students practice on accepted behaviors when "dining out"
- Focus students on environmental responsibility by using placemats, dishes and cutlery from home rather than disposable products

Sample Sign-up Sheet

Main Dishes and Salads
1.
2.
3.
4.
5.
6.
7.
8.

Desserts
1.
2.
3.
4.
5.
6.
7.
8.

Napkins
1.
2.

Punch Bowl
1.

Punch Ingredients
(2L clear pop or 1 L juice)
1.
2.
3.
4.
5.
6.
7.
8.

- Provide an opportunity for students to broaden their experience with eating different types of food
- Allow the sharing of family traditions when ethnic foods are brought in
- Give students "hands-on" experience with a unit of study
- Showcase student talents when "entertainment" is part of a potluck
- Promote creativity and respect for diversity

Ideas for Potlucks

Unit of Study	Potluck Theme
Solar System/Space Exploration	Alien Appetites
Immigration	Multicultural Theme
Friendship	Friendship Salad
Nutrition	Healthy Choices
Environment	Everything GREEN

Celebrating Events and Achievements

In addition to celebrating the attainment of class goals and being part of a group, students also enjoy activities that celebrate the special aspects of that particular school year and the special achievements of members of the class. Some of these types of celebrations are ongoing, but many take place at the end of the year. Here are a couple of my favorites.

Class Photo Album

A class photo album, assembled over the course of a school year, provides a wonderful record of the events and activities of that year. Students enjoy adding to it to celebrate their many achievements and special moments throughout the year.

In addition to the benefits for my current class, I have found that a class photo album from the previous year provides a starting point for excellent suggestions at class meetings of ideas that have been tried in previous years, as students see photos of events in the old albums.

To assemble and maintain a class photo album:

- Take photos during the year of your students working and playing together
- Get doubles made, so you can give one to students to put into their learning journal, and keep the other to go into the class photo album
- Ask a couple of interested students to keep the album up to date and to write captions or explanations to go with the photos
- Crop photos where possible so that they take up less room
- Write the school year on the front of the album or on the spine
- Glue a class photo on the inside cover, with a list of student names
- Keep albums from year to year, as part of your bookshelf, for current students to leaf through

Spoof Awards

In some schools, end-of-term or end-of-year awards are given to outstanding students in areas such as academics, athletics and citizenship. Why not recognize the abilities of all students in your class in a fun way? At the last class meeting of the year, encourage students to bring "spoof" awards they have made for classmates. These are meant to be amusing, but positive, recognitions of an individual student's strengths or accomplishments, or can focus on a particular event, often humorous, which the student is known for that has occurred during the year.

To facilitate such an event:

- Discuss the idea of awards with students at a class meeting. Suggest that everyone needs to be recognized by others, and that this activity is an opportunity to do this.
- Reminisce about events and situations that have happened during the term or year, and recall funny incidents that you have shared.
- Brainstorm a list of possible things people could be given an award for, and make up titles for these awards (e.g., "The Below-the-Bar Award" for the person who got down the lowest doing the Limbo at the school dances).
- Arrange for names to be drawn out of a hat. These are kept secret, but you will need to record them.
- Give students a week to work on an award for the person they have drawn. Tell students that the certificate or award must state the name of the award, as well as the reason it is being given.
- Decide with the class whether the awards will be written on a certificate, put on a ribbon (primary students can wear these to an assembly), or if they will be construction projects. The latter allows for a great deal of creativity!
- Have each student present the award to the person he or she has made it for at the final class meeting. Begin with one student, then have the recipient become the next presenter. If your school has a school-wide assembly to present awards, the spoof awards can be given out in your classroom before going to the assembly, so each child feels especially important that day.

Things I Like About ...

Our high schools have yearbooks, into which students write comments to their friends as a keepsake souvenir. Not having yearbooks in the elementary school, this end-of-year activity in their learning journals serves as a "yearbook" entry and gives positive encouragement to each person in the class. It is a thoughtful activity, where students quietly reflect upon what each member of the class has meant to them.

To facilitate the activity:

- Suggest the idea at a class meeting. Tell the class that this is a wonderful way to "celebrate" the encouragements that they have been giving each other all year in class meetings.
- Have the students print their name to complete the sentence "Things I Like About _____" and to make it span two pages in their journal.
- Suggest that they add a decorative border around the pages and color the title and border.
- Explain to students that the comments they write in other students' books must be positive in nature. Encouraging comments can focus on what they have noticed about what a student is good at, or has improved in, personality traits, or aspects of a student that are appreciated.
- Pass out a class list for each student, so they can keep track of whose book they have written in.
- Direct students to pass the journals around the room until everyone has made a comment about everyone else. This will take a fair amount of time, perhaps as much as an hour.
- Invite the students to read what others have written about them. Discuss the activity together.

Final Reflections on Class Meetings

Class meetings make the class a better place to be—same with school.

Student, age 10

Class meetings, such as those described in this book, have many benefits and far-reaching effects. You will notice these benefits more and more as time passes, and you and the students have enjoyed many effective meetings, as well as preparatory and spin-off activities.

There will be a difference in the tone of your class, particularly in the way students deal with each other and with their problems. There will be an increased enthusiasm for school, leading some students to enjoy school for the first time. Many students will improve in their ability to express their feelings, talk about issues and make decisions. They will become more comfortable speaking in front of each other and in front of larger groups. They will become more accountable and more responsible, and the number of problems in the class will greatly diminish. Finally, you will all have a lot of fun together doing things the students have planned.

Participating in class meetings sets students up to be successful. When students see themselves as valuable contributors to the classroom, taking ownership and responsibility, and receiving positive recognition from their peers, they feel good about themselves. Students who feel good about themselves are more able to make good choices for their behavior and for their academic learning. As one ten year old concludes, *I would say that class meetings are very important because it helps kids be better kids. Kids learn to be more responsible and that's good. Class meetings lets everybody be equal, including the teacher.*

Professional Resources

Bellanca, James and Robin Fogarty. *Catch Them Thinking: A Handbook of Classroom Strategies.* Arlington Heights, IL: IRI Skylight, 1986.

Brownlie, Faye and Judith King. *Learning in Safe Schools: Creating Classrooms Where All Students Belong.* Markham, ON: Pembroke Publishers, 2000.

Child Development Project. *Ways We Want Our Class to Be: Class Meetings That Build Commitment to Kindness and Learning.* Oakland, CA: Developmental Studies Center, 1996.

Coles, Robert. *The Moral Intelligence of Children.* New York: Random House, 1977.

Cramer, R. H. "Clear the Air with Class Meetings." *Learning,* July/August 1988, 59-61.

Dinkmeyer, D., McKay, G. D., and Dinkmeyer, D. Jr. *Systematic Training for Effective Teaching.* Circle Pines, MN: American Guidance Service, 1980.

Gabarino, J. "Educating Children in a Socially Toxic Environment." *Educational Leadership,* 54, April 1997, 12-16.

Glasser, W. *The Quality School: Managing Students without Coercion.* (2nd ed.) New York: Harper Perennial, 1990.

Goleman, D. *Emotional Intelligence: Why It Can Matter More Than IQ.* New York: Bantam, 1995.

Jensen, E. *Teaching with the Brain in Mind.* Alexandria, Virginia: Association for Supervision and Curriculum Development, 1998.

Johnson, D. W. and Johnson, R. T. *Teaching Students to Be Peacemakers.* Edina, MN: Interaction Book, 1991.

Kohn, A. *Beyond Discipline: From Compliance to Community.* Alexandria, VA: Association for Supervision and Curriculum Development, 1996.

Lions Club International and Quest International. *Changes and Challenges: Becoming the Best You Can Be.* (3rd ed.) Newark, Ohio: Quest International, 1985.

Pippus, J. and Benson, D. (Producers) *Bridgette: The Power of Class Meetings.* (Videotape), 1999—available from School District #83, Box 129, Salmon Arm, BC, Canada V1E 4N2.

Schneider, E. "Giving Students a Voice in the Classroom." *Educational Leadership,* 53, September 1996, 22-26.

Sergiovanni, R. J. *Moral Leadership: Getting to the Heart of School Improvement.* San Francisco, CA: Jossey-Bass, 1992.

www.sd83.bc.ca (Class Meetings). School District #83 Web site, Salmon Arm, BC, Canada.

Index

Acknowledgments

My personal journey toward creating democratic, respectful classroom communities began long ago with the birth of our first child and an Adlerian parenting course. Since that time, I have met and worked with many people along the way who have made the journey not only educational, but also exhilarating.

Thanks to Madge, who taught me how to incorporate higher-level thinking into my teaching, and to Judy, our "local pioneer" of brain-based learning. Thanks also to Ken, a principal who truly modeled and mentored. To the staff of Beairsto Elementary in the late eighties, *merci mille fois pour votre acceptance et support*—and your fun and laughter—during the most challenging period of my career.

The path of my journey widened, and in the early 1990s, I arrived at a huge gathering of minds and ideas that both cemented and enriched my beliefs about education. Thanks to Susan Close and Faye Brownlie and associates, for sharing with us your wealth of strategies that engage the learner. To the staff of Highland Park School in the early nineties—wow! Wasn't that an exciting ride! I remember the staffroom being alive with "teacher talk" in those years, as together, we investigated, analyzed and modified new insights and ideas. Many of the ideas and strategies listed in Chapters 5 and 6 of this resource came out of those years at Highland Park and were shared by many, making their origin difficult to pinpoint. Where possible, I have given credit to specific people for an idea, but for the rest, I hope that if the originator of a concept is reading this, they know I am acknowledging their creativity and thanking them for the richness and depth their ideas have added to my teaching.

To Karen, for your "beigeness," and to Petra, for your "va-va-voomness"— we were a great team. And to Rea, for your wisdom. To the students in my Grade 4/5 class at Highland Park Elementary (1998-99) and my Grade 5/6 class at Len Wood Elementary (1999-2000), thank you for your reflections and your valuable input. To Janine, Faye and Emily—thanks for your memories. And to Shelly, thank you for helping me through the writing of the original handbook with your illustrations and thoughtfulness.

The journey continues, and in the past few years, some sideroads have been taken that have led to wonderful things. Thanks, Dawn, for leading me down those pathways. Thank you for your vision, your intuition and your trust. And John—thank you for your ability to analyze, capsulize and create. You make it look so good.

While on the path of my professional journey, another road has run parallel. To my friends, thank you for your patience and understanding during these past few years. I'm back! And to my family, whose continued encouragement and support allows me to do great things. To Geoff, who taught me the importance of having "balance." To Melanie, who taught me about compassion and caring, and to Mel, who helps put it all in perspective. Thank you for the enriched life that we share—the delightful discussions, the laughter and the love.

Bridgette: The Power of Class Meetings

This 15 minute VHS format video demonstrates the power of a weekly class meeting in helping students make responsible decisions and problem solve effectively. Donna Styles' class is the focus of this video and the video can be freely reproduced for educational purposes.

To order your copy or for more information, contact:

Clare Meunier c/o Education Department
School District #83, Box 129, Salmon Arm, B.C. V1E 4N2
E-mail at educ2@sd83.bc.ca; Telephone 1-250-804-7826